English Matters!

Series Consultant
WILLIAM STRONG, Ph.D.
Department Head and Professor of Secondary Education
Director, Utah Writing Project
Utah State University

Advisers
BEVERLY ANN CHIN, Ph.D.
Former President of National Council of Teachers of English and
Professor of English
University of Montana

MARILEE FOGLESONG
Former Young Adult Coordinator
New York Public Library

Volume 9
self-assessment – synthesizing

GROLIER
EDUCATIONAL

SHERMAN TURNPIKE, DANBURY, CONNECTICUT 06816

Published 2000 by Grolier Educational
Sherman Turnpike
Danbury, CT 06816

Developed, Designed, and Produced by BOOK BUILDERS INCORPORATED
Cover design: Sherry Williams
Cover photography: Tilman Reitzle

SET ISBN: 0-7172-9437-4
VOLUME ISBN: 0-7172-9446-3

For information address the publisher:
Grolier Educational, Sherman Turnpike, Danbury, CT 06816

Library of Congress Cataloging-in-Publication Data

English matters!
     p. cm.
     Includes index.
     SUMMARY: A multi-volume English language textbook with alphabetically arranged entries on such topics as grammar, style, punctuation, and writing and research skills.
     ISBN 0-7172-9437-4 (set : alk. paper)
     1. English language—Rhetoric Handbooks, manuals, etc. 2. English language—Grammar Handbooks, manuals, etc. 3. English language—Usage Handbooks, manuals, etc. 4. Report writing Handbooks, manuals, etc. [1. English language—Rhetoric. 2. English language—Grammar. 3. English language—Usage 4. Report writing.] I. Grolier Educational (Firm)
PE1408 .E52 1999
428.2'4 —dc21
                                                                                    99-33249
                                                                                         CIP

Contents

Preface

The Purpose of *English Matters!*

Welcome to *English Matters!*—the one encyclopedia that helps with just about any matter you come across in English or language-arts classes, assignments, and tests. The ten-volume set sends you on your way to finding answers to questions about writing and speaking style, grammar, usage, and punctuation. Whatever question you have about English, you are likely to find the answer in *English Matters!*

Here are some example questions:

- SPELLING AND VOCABULARY: What's the **plural** of *potato*? of *patio*?
- WORDS COMMONLY CONFUSED: Should I write *affect* or *effect*?
- MECHANICS AND PUNCTUATION: Do I use two **punctuation** marks after this **abbreviation**?
- GRAMMAR AND USAGE: What does "**fragment**" written next to my sentence mean?
- PARTS OF SPEECH: What's a **relative pronoun** relative to?
- WRITING: What will make my **paragraph** of **description** more descriptive?
- THINKING SKILLS: Is a **logical jump** something good or something bad?
- LITERARY TERMS: How are **sonnets** different from other poems?
- SPEAKING/LISTENING: Where can I find how to perform **readers' theater**?
- RESEARCH: How do I make a **bibliography** for my paper?
- TEST-TAKING: Where can I find out about **college-entrance tests**?

Use *English Matters!* to look up any of the dark, or boldfaced, words from the list of questions, and you will find the answers.

Looking Things Up

Each boldfaced term from the preceding list is called a **key word**. The key words appear in alphabetical order, A to Z, in the appropriate volume of *English Matters!* and in the set index at the back of each of the ten vol-

umes. Alongside each key word in the ten volumes, you will find either an entry—definition, simple explanation, and lots of examples—or a cross-reference to an alternative key word and entry.

The pages with blue side borders call attention to the most important key words, to those that are the building blocks for everything you do with English. To be successful in life, you need to know the meaning of these terms—and how to follow, bend, and even break the rules related to them. For example, you need to know when you *must* use a comma and when the choice is up to you, when you should not split an infinitive and when it is okay to do so.

Although rules are important, the more than one thousand entries in *English Matters!* go beyond the rules of English. You'll find helpful examples of concepts like **noun** and **narrative**. And you'll find interesting graphics—everything from the layout for a **business letter** to illustrations of a **pie chart** and a **Venn diagram**.

In the margins are useful boxes of at-a-glance information: **Checklist** summarizes steps in a process; **Helpful Hint** short-circuits errors; **Memory Jogger** distinguishes homonyms; **Net Source** helps to locate reliable Internet sites; **Punctuation Pointer** reinforces the mechanics of writing; and **Word Check** will help increase your vocabulary. One more feature—**For Further Reading**—suggests other sources of interest to students your age.

Our cross-referencing of key words makes your research easier by showing you how interconnected hundreds of terms are. The cross-references appear in small capitalized type, either in the entry itself (as for the term QUOTATION in the entry for **capitalization**) or in the margin under the label *See also* (as for the term SPELLING in the entry for **comparative degree**).

English Matters! offers you the engaging facts and practical advice to help you do well in what really matters—your professional and personal future. We encourage you to ask questions often and to turn to *English Matters!* for answers.

William Strong, Ph.D.
Series Consultant

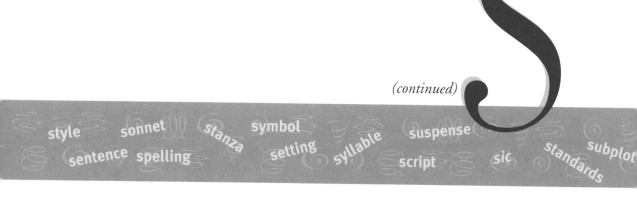

self-assessment An important part of learning in which you evaluate your own work to see if you have met expectations. Usually, self-assessment involves PERFORMANCE ASSESSMENT. That is, instead of giving yourself a **multiple-choice test** and scoring it, you must evaluate a product you've created by going through a process.

Self-assessment gives you the chance to reflect on what you've learned from an assignment, what new questions you may have formed based on what you've learned, what your strengths and weaknesses are in completing an assignment, and what you might do better (or as well as) on your next assignment.

You self-assess your writing in a number of ways. In a whole-class setting or during a teacher conference (see CONFERENCING) *informal* self-assessment may be as simple as reflecting on and then answering aloud your teacher's questions about an assignment. You may also informally assess your writing when you discuss it with another student during PEER EDITING. Given your peer's responses to your writing, how do you think you've done on that piece of writing, compared with a piece from, say, last month? In *formal* self-assessment you can use checklists that remind you of everything from DEVELOPMENT to MECHANICS.

At times you may write a reflective essay as the final part of a larger assignment. Your teacher may ask you to answer specific questions (for example, "How did I carry out each step of the WRITING PROCESS?" "What do I need to spend more time on next time?") or more open-ended questions (for example, "How has this assignment helped me improve my writing?").

See also

CONNOTATION

JARGON

SLANG

semantics The science, or study, of words and meanings. Semantics deals with more than what a DICTIONARY offers about a word and its meanings. As a listener or reader you may know the dictionary readings of every word in every SENTENCE you hear or read but may still not know what the speaker or writer *means—what he or she is trying to communicate.* If you have ever thought or said, "What is this writer talking about?" or "What's really going on here?" you have touched on the field called semantics. Similarly, if you're having trouble figuring out if "We'll discuss this matter later" is a well-intended promise or a dire warning, you have had first-hand experience with semantics.

Another way of looking at semantics is to say it tries to explain *how* a word has a meaning that various people can agree on and communicate about. Linguists who work with semantics claim that words get agreed-upon meanings in one of three ways—(1) through reference to something observed (this approach works for the word *chair*); (2) through verification (this approach helps people understand attributes, such as what is meant by *wet*); and (3) through use or context (this approach helps people understand ABSTRACT NOUNS such as *beauty* and slippery VERBS such as *is* and *are*). But understanding each other continues to be one of the most demanding of human pursuits.

semi/bi *See* BI/SEMI

semicolon PUNCTUATION mark (;) used to connect SENTENCE elements of equal grammatical weight.

Use a semicolon to join two closely related INDEPENDENT CLAUSES not joined by a coordinating CONJUNCTION.

> The dog felt hot; his tongue stuck out.

Use a semicolon to join INDEPENDENT CLAUSES linked by a conjunctive ADVERB (for example, *furthermore, instead, therefore*) or transitional expression (for example, *even so, in fact, on the other hand*) (see TRANSITION).

> I'm sick; thus I can't go swimming.

Usually, COMMAS separate items in a series, but you can use semicolons between elements in a series if the individual elements themselves contain commas.

> I like cake, pie, and cookies; cats, dogs, and hamsters; and television, radio, and movies.

Use a comma, not a semicolon, between a DEPENDENT CLAUSE and the rest of a sentence.

> If you don't go, I'll scream.

sensory detail DETAIL added to writing to appeal to one or more of the five senses: taste, touch, smell, hearing, and sight. Use sensory detail in DESCRIPTION to create images for your readers. The resulting IMAGERY will help your readers imagine the people, places, and events in your work.

See also

Punctuation Pointer

A sentence begins with a CAPITAL LETTER; it ends with a PERIOD, QUESTION MARK, or EXCLAMATION POINT.

Net Source

For more examples of how clauses and sentences work, see <http://owl.english.purdue.edu/files/Sentences.html>.

SENTENCE The sentence is the building block of all writing. Correspondence, articles, literature, and diaries all consist of sentences. A sentence must

1. have a SUBJECT and a PREDICATE
2. express a complete thought.

The following group of words meets the two requirements for a sentence:

SUBJECT ——————— PREDICATE ——————
Mark McGwire hit his sixty-first home run on his father's sixty-first birthday.

[expresses a complete idea]

The following groups of words meet one but not both requirements for a sentence.

	SUBJECT
NOT A SENTENCE	The player waving to the crowd. [missing predicate]

	SUBJECT PREDICATE
NOT A SENTENCE	When the player came to bat. [contains a subject and a predicate but is not a complete thought]

The preceding word group about the player is a DEPENDENT CLAUSE (also called a SUBORDINATE CLAUSE), which depends on, or needs, something else to be a complete thought.]

Purposes of sentences

A sentence usually has one of four purposes.

1. A **declarative sentence** makes a statement.

   I'll be home by nine o'clock.

2. An **interrogative sentence** asks a question.

   Will you be home by nine o'clock?

3. An **imperative sentence** gives a command or makes a request.

   Be home by nine o'clock.

4. An **exclamatory sentence** expresses feeling.

   Ugh, I have to be home by nine o'clock!

Structures of Sentences

A sentence is classified according to the number and kinds of CLAUSES it has.

1. A **simple sentence** has one MAIN CLAUSE (also called an INDEPENDENT CLAUSE) and no SUBORDINATE (or DEPENDENT) clauses.

   I will be home by nine o'clock.

2. A **compound sentence** has two or more MAIN CLAUSES but no SUBORDINATE CLAUSES.

   I have to be home at nine, but you can stay out until ten.

3. A **complex sentence** has one MAIN CLAUSE and one or more SUBORDINATE CLAUSES.

   Because I must do a report, I must be home by nine.

4. A **compound-complex** sentence has two or more MAIN CLAUSES and one or more SUBORDINATE CLAUSES.

   I have to be home by nine, but you can stay out until ten because you're older.

Helpful Hint

Sentence Test

Put the expression *It is true that* in front of a word group you are wondering about. If the result makes sense, then the original word group is a sentence; if the result is meaningless, then the original word group doesn't qualify as a sentence.

It is true that Mark McGwire hit his sixty-first home run on his father's sixty-first birthday. [sounds OK; is a sentence]

It is true that when the player came to bat. [doesn't sound right; not a sentence]

---

sentence combining Transforming basic SENTENCE constructions into more complicated structures. Sentence combining during EDITING helps you write tighter, more readable sentences. Though creating a longer sentence from shorter ones doesn't always improve your writing, sentence combining can help you get rid of unnecessary words, leading to more focused sentences. Sentence combining also helps you become comfortable manipulating sentence structure, thereby giving you more control of your writing.

Combined sentences can be *enjoined* or *embedded.* Enjoining sentences puts two sentences together with CONJUNCTIONS like *or, and,* or *but.* In the following examples sentences 1 and 2 are joined to form sentence 3, the combined sentence.

1. Andy dribbled the ball down the court.
2. Andy sank the jump shot.
3. Andy dribbled the ball down the court and sank the jump shot.

Embedded sentences combine two or more sentences by enveloping one into the other.

1. Nina's car careened off the road.
2. Julia screamed.
3. When Nina's car careened off the road, Julia screamed.

Embedding sentences can require more than one step. In the following examples sentences 1 and 2 are combined by embedding (see sentence 3) and are then tightened in sentence 4 to create a better construction.

1. The boy is rude.
2. The boy is taunting the teacher.

3. The boy who is taunting the teacher is rude.
4. The rude boy is taunting the teacher.

1. The robin is fat.
2. The robin is hopping around the front yard.
3. The robin that is hopping around the front yard is fat.
4. The fat robin is hopping around the front yard.

sentence, parts of A SENTENCE is composed of two main parts: a SUBJECT, which names who or what the sentence is about, and a PREDICATE, which describes the action performed by or state of being of the subject.

See also

CLAUSE

SENTENCE COMBINING

PHRASE

The Subject

The **complete subject** includes the SIMPLE SUBJECT—which is always a NOUN, PRONOUN, or noun substitute—and all its MODIFIERS.

SIMPLE SUBJECT
That large, lazy dog of mine sleeps all day.

You find the simple subject by asking Who? or What? about the VERB. In the previous example, who sleeps all day? The dog. So *dog* is the simple subject. Every other word in the complete subject modifies *dog*.

A sentence may have a COMPOUND SUBJECT—that is, two or more simple subjects joined by a coordinating CONJUNCTION.

Mom and Dad went shopping.

In an IMPERATIVE, or command, SENTENCE, the subject is understood to be *you*.

[You] Go home!

The Predicate

The **complete predicate** consists of one or more VERBS plus any modifiers or COMPLEMENTS.

> That large, lazy dog of mine sleeps all day.
>
> VERB (above *sleeps all day*)

In the previous example, the INTRANSITIVE VERB *sleeps* is modified by the phrase *all day*, which explains *when* the dog sleeps. The verb plus the modifier constitutes the complete predicate.

The SIMPLE PREDICATE of a sentence is either a single verb (such as *sleeps*) or a VERB PHRASE (such as *has been sleeping*).

Like subjects, verbs can be compound. Two or more verbs can take the same subject.

> My dog sleeps and eats.

Complements

A PREDICATE NOMINATIVE, a type of SUBJECT COMPLEMENT, is a noun or pronoun explaining or identifying the subject of a sentence.

> That car is a lemon.

A PREDICATE ADJECTIVE is another subject complement—one that modifies, or describes, the subject of the sentence.

> That car is blue.

Objects are another type of complement. The DIRECT OBJECT of a verb is a noun or pronoun that receives the action of the verb or shows the result of the action. It answers the questions *Whom?* or *What?*

> That dog bit Dad!

A direct object is sometimes followed by an OBJEC-TIVE COMPLEMENT, which renames or describes the direct object and thus completes its meaning.

> Our dog makes Dad <u>angry</u>.

The INDIRECT OBJECT of a verb is a noun or pronoun that precedes a direct object. The indirect object usually answers the question *to* whom/what? or *for* whom/what?

> Mom gave <u>me</u> a new chore.

Order of Sentence Elements

Most English sentences follow the pattern of subject/verb/complement (SVC) or subject/verb/object (SVO). Many do not.

The subject of a sentence does not always come before the predicate. *There is/was* or *There are/were* are EXPLETIVES that begin some (weak) sentences. In these sentences the subject follows the verb.

>   VERB   SUBJECT
> There *is* a new *car* in the garage.

Sometimes the subject and verb are inverted for effect.

>   VERB   SUBJ
> Glorious *is* the *day* in which the sun shines.

Glorious is an ADJECTIVE modifying *day;* it is not the subject of the sentence.

Finally, an INTERROGATIVE, or question, SENTENCE often sandwiches the subject between parts of a verb phrase.

> VERB   SUBJECT   VERB
> *Is* the *dog* still *howling*?

If you turn this question into a statement, the usual order returns.

>   SUBJECT   VERB
> The *dog is howling*.

— Helpful Hint —

Varying Sentence Beginnings

In REVISING and EDITING your compositions, try every once in a while to change a sentence so that it breaks the SVC or SVO pattern.

---

sentence fragment *See* FRAGMENT

sentence structure *See* SENTENCE; SYNTAX

sequence *See* CHRONOLOGICAL ORDER; DIRECTIONS

series comma Each COMMA used between items in a series of three or more words, PHRASES, or CLAUSES. No one debates the necessity for a comma between the first two items of a three-item series or between the first two items and between the second and third items in a four-item series (and so on), as illustrated by the extra-large commas in the examples below.

> THREE-ITEM SERIES: Joan **,** David, and Mark were all late.
> FOUR-ITEM SERIES: Joan **,** David **,** Mark, and Lisa were all late.

Some writers consider the final comma in a series optional. That is, in the first example above they consider the comma after *David* and before *and* optional; in the second example they consider the comma after *Mark* and before *and* optional. In fact, many newspapers and other publications always leave out the comma after the next-to-the-last item in a series. However, leaving it out sometimes causes confusion, as the examples below demonstrate, so this encyclopedia reminds you that you will never be wrong to include the final comma.

> The chef often gives us a choice of broccoli **,** cauliflower **,** peas **,** and carrots.

Without the comma after *peas* a reader will not be able to tell if *peas* and *carrots* refers to two separate vegetables served individually or to a single mixed vegetable dish. As it now stands, the example makes it totally clear that the choice is among four vegetables. If the writer wants to make it perfectly clear that the choice is among three vegetables, he or she can use an additional **coordinate conjunction.**

> The chef often gives us a choice of broccoli, cauli-flower, **and** peas and carrots.

One more thing to remember about commas in series: Never place a comma before the first item in a series or after the final item.

> The flag is red, white, and blue.

set-off quotation *See* BLOCK QUOTATION; QUOTATION

set/sit Two commonly confused VERBS with different meanings. The PRINCIPAL PARTS of the TRANSITIVE VERB *set,* meaning "to put or place," are *set, set, setting,* and *set.*

> I will <u>set</u> the ball down.
> I <u>set</u> the ball down yesterday.
> I have <u>set</u> the ball down before.

The principal parts of the intransitive verb *sit,* meaning "to be seated," are *sit, sat, sitting,* and *sat.*

> I <u>sit</u> on the chair.
> I <u>sat</u> on the chair yesterday.
> I have <u>sat</u> on the chair before.

See also
IRREGULAR VERBS
HOMOGRAPH,
HOMONYM,
HOMOPHONE

Memory Jogger

Transitive verbs like *set* take DIRECT OBJECTS. Without an object, don't use set.

setting When and where a story or play takes place. Stories and plays must be located in space and time. The four elements of setting—location, weather, time period, and time span—vary in importance from story to story. Important settings demand thorough descriptions and should show a clear relationship to the story's PLOT.

In some stories, like FOLKTALES, the setting gets only brief attention because it doesn't contribute significantly to the story line. This type of setting is called a **backdrop setting.** In other stories the setting is described in detail because it is critical to the story line. This type of setting is called an **integral setting.** Both Natalie Babbitt's *Tuck Everlasting* and Katherine Paterson's *Bridge to Terabithia* have integral settings.

setting a purpose for reading A crucial step in determining *how* you will read a specific text.

Broadly, you read for two purposes: to take knowledge from a text and to enjoy or be otherwise emotionally affected. You can read *Romeo and Juliet* to learn about the father-daughter relationship so that you can answer an ESSAY QUESTION. Or you can read it to feel anguish over deeply divided loyalties. You can enhance either experience if you understand before you begin to read what you are trying to gain from the text.

Here is some advice for getting the most out of each type of reading experience. If you are reading for knowledge, you may want to use SCANNING and note taking (see NOTE CARD, NOTE) and to read only parts of the text, often out of order. If you are reading for pleasure, find a quiet place where you can be comfortable and concentrate without interruption for long periods.

sexist language *See* NONSEXIST LANGUAGE

shall/will Words now used interchangeably, though *shall* is more FORMAL. You will hear *shall* most commonly in polite questions, such as *Shall I pour you a cup of tea?* or in legalistic directions or suggestions, as in *The applicant shall submit a completed portfolio by December.*

sharing A SYNONYM for the PUBLISHING stage of the WRITING PROCESS. In this stage the AUTHOR makes his or her work public by encouraging others to read it. Sharing writing enables you to get valuable **feedback** from your AUDIENCE and helps you develop confidence in your writing.

You can share your work in many ways, some more informal than others. When you write a LETTER to your best friend, help create the class bulletin board, or post a story or poem in your classroom, you are sharing your work. Recording (on audiocassette or videocassette) something you've written, giving a speech at a school assembly, and participating in a poetry reading are also ways of sharing your writing. You can share work more formally by, for example, having it published in the school NEWSPAPER or literary magazine, in your local newspaper, or in a national POETRY magazine. The INTERNET offers publishing opportunities too.

shibboleth A test word or password used by a group of people to detect outsiders attempting to pass themselves off as members of the group.

According to the Bible, one ancient group of people pronounced the Hebrew word *shibboleth* (which means "torrent of water") with the beginning sound *sh*. The people in this group used pronunciation as a way to identify men from another tribe who were trying to escape. The escapees gave themselves away because they pronounced the word *shibboleth* with the beginning sound *s*, not *sh*.

See also
ACCENT (DIALECT)
DIALECT
JARGON
SLANG

Today the term *shibboleth* applies to any word or pronunciation—or even custom—that identifies you as a member of one group and not a member of another. In other words, *shibboleth,* which was once a test word, has become the NOUN that names all such test words, PHRASES, sayings, or customs.

shift, unnecessary   Inappropriately changing PRONOUN, POINT OF VIEW, or TENSE within a piece of writing.

Pronouns
Do not use two different pronouns to refer to one and the same person.

> UNNECESSARY SHIFT: If one practices writing, you will improve.
> CORRECTED: If one practices writing, one will improve.
> OR: If you practice writing, you will improve.

Point of View
Stay with one point of view. If you start writing a NARRATIVE in FIRST PERSON, do not suddenly switch to SECOND PERSON or THIRD PERSON.

> I remember my thirteenth birthday as though it was yesterday, but four years have passed. It was a birthday ~~you'll~~ I'll never forget.

Tenses
When you choose a tense for a piece of writing, keep using that tense throughout the composition. Shift into other tenses only if you are explaining a complicated sequence.

Hammurabi was a king of ancient Babylonia.

Hammurabi made laws for his people. The laws

protected

~~protect~~ people's rights

short-answer test A test that requires you, the test taker, to choose a correct answer from alternatives. It differs from other types of tests, such as an ESSAY, which requires you to produce or create a response. (Some people also use the label *short-answer test* for fill-in-the-blank questions, in which the answer, which the test taker must generate, is only a few words long.)

Short-answer tests are widely used not only in the classroom but also in standardized college-entrance tests, the written part of driver's-license tests, tests for certain career opportunities, and in other situations where the goal of the test is primarily to determine the test taker's recall of information: FACTS, definitions of terms, and the like.

See also

ACT
COLLEGE BOARD
PERFORMANCE ASSESSMENT
SAT
TEST-TAKING

Types of Short-Answer Test Questions

Several types of questions are common in short-answer tests.

True-False

This type of question makes a statement. You have to determine whether the statement is true or false. Sometimes, you must change false statements to true statements.

One key to successfully answering true-false questions is to look for words such as *all, every, always,* and *never,* which often (but not always) turn a statement into an untrue OVERGENERALIZATION.

Multiple Choice

This type of question presents you with alternative responses—usually three, four, or five. Only one of the responses correctly answers the question or completes a statement begun in the question. Sometimes, an incorrect response has an element of truth to it but is not the "best" response.

One key to successfully answering multiple-choice questions is to eliminate incorrect responses. Usually, at least one or two of the responses are clearly incorrect; one may even be nonsensical. By eliminating obviously incorrect responses, you increase your odds of selecting the correct response.

Matching

This type of question contains two columns. Typically the items in the first column are numbered, and the items in the second column are lettered. You must "match" the items in one column with those in the other by recording the correct letter next to the correct numbered item (or vice versa). Usually the lists are of equal length, and each answer is used only once.

The key with such matching questions is to match up the most obvious pairs first, thus narrowing the possibilities for those items about which you might be less certain. On some tests, though, one list is longer than the other, making it harder to answer by elimination of choices.

See also

GENRE

short story A relatively brief fictional (see FICTION) NARRATIVE written in PROSE.

Defining a Short Story

Most efforts to define the term *short story* fail, although most readers recognize a short story when they see one.

One way to define the term is by length. A short story could be as brief as five hundred words or as long as twenty thousand words. This word count would distinguish it from a NOVELLA, which might range from twenty thousand to fifty thousand words, and from a NOVEL, which is usually longer than fifty thousand words. These numbers, though, are arbitrary; in theory it would be possible for a short novel to be shorter than a long short story.

A better way to define *short story* is in terms of its elements and structure. Like a novel or novella, a short story includes the following elements: PLOT, CHARACTERS, SETTING, POINT OF VIEW, and THEME. But a short story's plot is usually less complicated than a novel's. The plot of a short story usually focuses on a single set of actions; the cast of characters is usually smaller, often centering on a single character; and the setting is usually restricted to a single locale.

In common with novels and novellas, short stories also include the structural components EXPOSITION, RISING ACTION, CONFLICT, COMPLICATIONS, CLIMAX, and FALLING ACTION (which includes a DÉNOUEMENT and a RESOLUTION). A novel or novella, however, is likely to have a series of complications, rising actions, and climaxes, a structure that might be visualized as a series of ascending waves, like this:

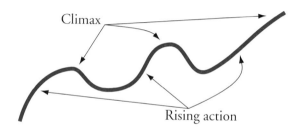

Furthermore, a novel is likely to use this narrative structure to trace actions that affect multiple characters or groups of characters; in other words, novels tend to have SUBPLOTS.

A short story, in contrast, will concentrate its impact on a single narrative wave, which might look more like this:

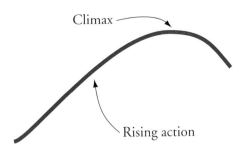

History of the Short Story

The roots of the short story lie with the tales and oral legends of preliterate times (see ORAL LITERATURE). Both fairy tales and the sophisticated tales written by Geoffrey Chaucer in the fourteenth century have many of the characteristics of short stories. However, as a distinct literary form the short story developed in the nineteenth century at the hands of American writers Nathaniel Hawthorne and Edgar Allan Poe, French writers Honoré Balzac and Guy de Maupassant, Russian writer Anton Chekov, and others. Major twentieth-century short story writers include O. Henry (who introduced the SURPRISE ENDING), James Joyce, Henry James, Ernest Hemingway, Katherine Anne Porter, Katherine Mansfield, Eudora Welty, and many others.

Example of a Short Story

Here is the beginning of a classic short story, "The Tell-Tale Heart" by Poe. The opening paragraphs begin to create the overall effect of this story—insanity of a kind.

Model

> True!—nervous—very, very dreadfully nervous I had been and am; but why *will* you say that I am mad? The disease had sharpened my senses—not destroyed—not dulled them. Above all was the sense of hearing acute. I heard all things in the heaven and in the earth. I heard many things in hell. How, then, am I mad? Hearken! And observe how healthily—how calmly I can tell you the whole story.
>
> It is impossible to say how first the idea entered my brain; but once conceived, it haunted me day and night. Object there was none. Passion there was none. I loved the old man. He had never wronged me. He had never given me insult. For his gold I had no desire. I think it was his eye! Yes, it was this! He had the eye of a vulture—a pale blue eye, with a film over it. Whenever it fell upon me, my blood ran cold; and so by degrees—very gradually—I made up my mind to take the life of the old man, and thus rid myself of the eye forever.
>
> Now this is the point. You fancy me mad. Madmen know nothing. But you have seen me. You should have seen how wisely I proceeded—with what cau-tion—with what foresight—with what dissimulation

> I went to work! I was never kinder to the old man than during the whole week before I killed him. And every night, about midnight, I turned the latch of his door and opened it—oh, so gently! And then, when I had made an opening sufficient for my head, I put in a dark lantern, all closed, closed, so that no light shone out, and then I thrust in my head. . . .

showing vs. telling Two types of writing statements that develop ideas and serve different purposes. Telling statements are general and give the reader a broad picture. Showing statements include specific DETAILS as EVIDENCE for the telling statements. In general, you should use more showing than telling statements in your writing.

sic A LATIN TERM that means "thus" or "so."

As a writer you may use *sic*—usually in ITALICS and square BRACKETS—in QUOTATIONS that have mistakes in GRAMMAR AND USAGE and in SPELLING. By placing [*sic*] immediately after the mistake, you signal to readers that the mistake was in the original, not in your transcription.

sight/cite/site *See* CITE/SIGHT/SITE

See also
COHERENCE
SUBORDINATION

signal word A word or PHRASE that lets readers know where a discussion or argument is heading. A signal word is similar to a TRANSITION.

Just as a street or highway system needs signs to point drivers in the right direction, a piece of writing (or a speech) needs signal words to help readers know where they are going. Some signal words and phrases point to *time* relationships: *next, then, afterwards, before.* Others point to the *opposition* of ideas: *but, although, on the other hand, in contrast, however.* Still others point to examples: *for example, for instance, such.* Some point to conclusions: *therefore, in conclusion, thus.* Finally, some signal words and phrases suggest *addition: and, in addition, also, another, as well as, plus, on top of that, moreover.*

sign, symbol In writing, a symbol is any mark that stands for a word. Common symbols include the AMPERSAND (&), the dollar sign ($), and the percent sign (%). *Sign* is more commonly used to refer to mathematical notation: minus sign (–), plus sign (+), equal sign (=). But *sign* and *symbol* are often used interchangeably.

signature Your typed signed name in a letter. In a business letter leave four line spaces after the complimentary CLOSING; then type your name as you intend to sign it. Sign the letter in blue or black ink above your typed name. Personal letters do not need to be signed as formally.

See also
E-MAIL
LETTER, BUSINESS
LETTER, FRIENDLY

silent *e* At the end of a written word, an *e* that is "silent" (not pronounced) but that changes the pronunciation of an earlier VOWEL and sometimes of the letters *th*.

See also
SILENT LETTER

The silent *e* is part of the SPELLING of a large number of English words. Common examples include *bite, breathe, note, fate,* and *cute.*

While the final *e* in each of the preceding words is not pronounced, its presence changes the pronunciation of the earlier vowel or vowels, which come between CONSONANTS, from "short" to "long." Thus, the word "bit" is pronounced /bit/, to rhyme with *hit* and *sit.* The *i* is short because there is no final, silent *e.* Adding *e* changes the pronunciation to /bīt/; the *i* is now long, so the word rhymes with *kite* and *might*.

These final *e*'s were not always silent. In the MIDDLE ENGLISH spoken hundreds of years ago, a word such as *bite* was two SYLLABLES; speakers pronounced the *e* so that the word would have sounded like "BI-tah."

silent letter A letter that is part of the SPELLING of a word but that is not pronounced.

One reason that English spelling is so difficult is that a large number of letters are silent. These letters are part of spelled words because when these words entered the language and were written down centuries ago (see OLD ENGLISH, MIDDLE ENGLISH), every letter *was* pronounced. While pronunciation has changed, spelling has tended to remain fixed. Another source of silent letters is borrowings from other languages; the spelling has been retained, but the pronunciation has been adapted for the ears of English speakers. Complicating matters is the large number of DIALECTS of English spoken throughout the world. Because of these dialects the pronunciation of many words is not uniform.

Many letters can be silent in a given word. Here are some common examples.

1. The *p* before an *n* in such words as *pneumonia* and *pneumatic*
2. The *w* before *r* in many words, including *write, wring, wrinkle, wren, wrench,* and *wreck*
3. The *k* before *n* in such words as *knight, knee,* and *knowledge*
4. The *gh* in such words as *knight, might, sight, neighbor,* and *light*

5. The *h* in such words as *ghost, rhubarb, rhythm, khaki, while,* and *ghoul*
6. The *g* before an *n* in such words as *gnat, impugn,* and *reign*
7. The *b* in such words as *climb* or *tomb*
8. The *m* in a word such as *mnemonic*

simile A **figure of speech** (or FIGURATIVE LANGUAGE) in which two otherwise dissimilar objects or ideas are compared, using such words as *like* and *as*. Don't confuse a simile with a METAPHOR, which also compares dissimilar things but does so by equating them. Thus, while a simile says that "X is like Y," a metaphor says that "X is Y."

You will frequently encounter similes in POETRY, which relies heavily on figurative language to create imaginative effects. But you will also find similes in FICTION, DRAMA, and NONFICTION as well. Any writer is likely to use a simile to explain an idea, illuminate a concept, or enrich the reader's understanding by showing an underlying similarity between two otherwise dissimilar things.

Some similes are part of our everyday VOCABULARY and have become CLICHÉS. Examples include "pretty as a picture," "you look like a million bucks," or "busy as a bee." More imaginative writers, though, create similes that enable readers to see things in new ways. In Act II of Shakespeare's *Romeo and Juliet,* Juliet, professes her love to Romeo with a simile.

Model

> My bounty is as boundless as the sea,
> My love as deep.

The English poet Gerard Manley Hopkins (1844–1889) was known for his vivid similes, as in "God's Grandeur":

Model

> The world is charged with the
> grandeur of God.
> > It will flame out, like shining
> > from shook foil;
> > It gathers to a greatness, like
> > the ooze of oil
> Crushed. . . .

Remember that the word *like* does not necessarily signal a simile. In the sentence "My house is like your house" there is no simile because two like objects are being compared.

See also

AGREEMENT, SUBJECT-
 VERB
INVERTED SENTENCE
TENSE

simple predicate The part of a PREDICATE that consists only of the VERB or VERB PHRASE.

Sentences contain two major parts. The SUBJECT is the "actor" or "topic" of the sentence. The predicate says something about the subject. Together, the subject and predicate form a complete sentence. The **complete predicate** consists of all the words in the predicate, not only the verb or verb phrase, but also a SUBJECT COMPLEMENT, a DIRECT OBJECT, an INDIRECT OBJECT, and an ADVERB or other MODIFIER. The simple predicate is only the verb or verb phrase. A simple predicate may contain two or more verbs, or a COMPOUND VERB.

> My teacher <u>wrote</u> a book.
> He <u>has written</u> four others.

> By the end of next year he <u>will</u>
>   <u>have written</u> six books and
>   <u>planned</u> two others.

simple sentence *See* DECLARATIVE SENTENCE; SENTENCE; TECHNICAL WRITING; VARYING SENTENCE BEGINNINGS, LENGTHS

simple subject The NOUN or PRONOUN that is the SUBJECT of a SENTENCE.

A sentence consists of two main parts. One is the subject, which is the "actor" or the "topic" of the sentence. The other is the PREDICATE, which says something about the subject. Together the subject and predicate make up a complete sentence.

The **complete subject** contains all the words in the subject—not only the noun or pronoun but also ADJECTIVES, ADJECTIVE CLAUSES, APPOSITIVES, and any other words or PHRASES that modify the subject (see MODIFIER). The simple subject contains only the main word or words that are part of the complete subject. A simple subject may contain two (or more) nouns or pronouns, or a COMPOUND SUBJECT.

> The soaring <u>mountains</u> of the West are a good vaca-
>   tion destination.
> The <u>Rocky Mountains</u>, which we visited last summer,
>   are breathtaking.
> The <u>mountains</u> and <u>streams</u> were relaxing.

simple tenses *See* FUTURE TENSE; PAST TENSE; PRESENT TENSE

single quotation mark *See* QUOTATION MARK

singular The form of a NOUN, PRONOUN, or VERB that indicates "one."

Most nouns can be singular or PLURAL: *tool/tools, man/men*. Some nouns are normally always singular: *honesty, truthfulness*. PERSONAL PRONOUNS other than *you* distinguish singular and plural: *I/we, he/they*. Most INDEFINITE PRONOUNS are singular: *anyone, everyone*. In the PRESENT TENSE, THIRD-PERSON singular SUBJECTS take the singular form of the verb: *He sits*.

site/cite/sight *See* CITE/SIGHT/SITE

sit/set *See* SET/SIT

situational irony *See* IRONY

sketch A brief DESCRIPTION, as in a CHARACTER SKETCH, or an initial draft (see DRAFTING) of a composition, as an OUTLINE. A sketch can also describe a brief, light piece of writing that resembles a SHORT STORY or ESSAY but that is intentionally not serious.

skimming A READING technique in which the reader rapidly glances through a text (a book, an article, a SHORT STORY, an ENCYCLOPEDIA entry, and so on) for its central ideas.

Skimming is a good way to preview (or review) a piece of writing. In skimming you glance rapidly through the work, looking for titles, headings, and BOLDFACE terms and quickly reading the TOPIC SENTENCES of PARAGRAPHS. The purpose is to gain an overview of the content before beginning more detailed study. By skimming, you grasp the most important points before absorbing the details and other supporting material.

Skimming is also a useful technique in conducting research. Skimming a book or article rather than closely reading it will give you a better sense of its usefulness for your research topic. Skim first; if appropriate, read later.

Skimming is similar to SCANNING in that both refer to a rapid overview of the work. But while you skim to grasp the overall topic or subject matter, you scan to locate a specific idea or piece of information.

skit A short, self-contained dramatic or comic presentation put on for a particular PURPOSE: For instance, you might create a skit to condense or summarize information, make a point about an idea learned, or present a key SCENE from a NOVEL.

slang INFORMAL words and PHRASES that are used by particular social groups, often so that other people will be unable to fully understand them.

The term *slang* is difficult to define precisely, partly because it overlaps with other, related terms. One such term is COLLOQUIALISM, which refers generally to the kind of informal speech nearly everyone uses in everyday conversation or in, for example, a friendly letter (see LETTER, FRIENDLY).

Another related term is JARGON. While this term refers to the language of a group, it tends to refer to the specialized VOCABULARY shared by members of professions, hobby or recreational groups, or the like. Thus, lawyers use jargon, but so do horse fanciers, auto enthusiasts, golfers, and other groups whose members share a common vocabulary—which might include slang.

The relationship among these terms might be represented by overlapping circles:

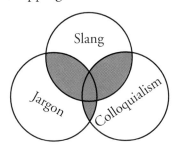

Another reason *slang* is hard to define is that it is constantly shifting and changing. Slang identifies its users as a member of a social group. Part of its purpose is for members to have a common "lingo" that excludes nonmembers. For this reason teenagers use slang frequently, since slang is likely to exclude—and perhaps even shock—the adult community. But as the words catch on and find their way into the speech of the general population, they lose their power to exclude and include, so they are abandoned and new words take their place.

Probably the best way to define slang is by example. One of the most persistent slang words is the all-purpose *cool,* meaning "good." But while *cool* has enjoyed a long lifespan after originating with jazz musicians in the 1920s and 1930s, it is the exception. Most slang catches on and then disappears with last year's popular movie or hit record. In the 1960s, for example, something that was cool was *far out* or *groovy.* These words gave up their place to *awesome* and *radical,* which in turn were replaced by *sweet* and even *bad.*

Whether you use slang or not depends on your AUDIENCE. Clearly you should avoid slang in FORMAL writing assignments, unless the slang term is critical to the point you are making. Then you might consider defining it for reader not already familiar with it.

slant rhyme *See* CONSONANCE; RHYME

slash A PUNCTUATION mark (/), often referred to as a virgule or SOLIDUS, that has a number of specific functions in writing.

See also
NONSEXIST LANGUAGE

1. **Fractions:** Use the slash to divide the numerator and denominator in numerical fractions: *9/16 drill bit.* The slash is also part of the percent sign (%).

2. **Abbreviations:** Use the slash in certain ABBREVIATIONS such as *c/o* ("care of," used in addresses), *A/1C* ("airman first class"), *I/O* ("input/output"), and sometimes *a/k/a* ("also known as," referring to an alias).

3. **Poetry:** Use the slash to separate lines of POETRY when you are running them into the text:

Model

> When Romeo first sees Juliet on the balcony, he says, "But soft, what light through yonder window breaks? / It is the east, and Juliet is the sun."

4. **Alternatives:** The slash is used in a SENTENCE with paired alternatives such as "The character's name is Victor/Victoria." Some people use *he/she* and *his/her* in their writing to avoid sexist language.

5. **URLs:** The slash separates parts of INTERNET addresses.

Slavic Languages *See* BALTO-SLAVIC LANGUAGES, INFLUENCE ON ENGLISH

ALLEN PARK PUBLIC LIBRARY

slow/slowly *Slow* is the ADJECTIVE, so it is used to modify a NOUN. *Slowly* is an ADVERB, so it is used to modify a VERB or an adjective. In INFORMAL LANGUAGE *slow* is widely accepted as an adverb: *You should drive <u>slow</u> on this curvy road.* In FORMAL LANGUAGE, however, use the adverb form when you're modifying a verb, adjective, or other adverb.

> My horse is too <u>slow</u>.
> The <u>slow</u> horse tried my patience.
> The horse goes too <u>slowly</u>.

A similar distinction applies to other commonly used adjective/adverb pairs, including *quick/quickly* and *loud/loudly.*

solidus Another name for the PUNCTUATION mark often called a SLASH. Use it to separate paired words presented as alternatives.

> The choice is of *colour/color.*
> Have you read the entry *affect/effect?*

soliloquy A type of MONOLOGUE in which a CHARACTER in a DRAMA voices his or her thoughts directly to the AUDIENCE. Often the character is onstage alone; if other characters are present, they remain silent.

Soliloquies were common in the drama of the sixteenth, seventeenth, and eighteenth centuries. The writer who used the soliloquy most artfully was Shakespeare. Some of the most famous lines in Shakespeare's plays come from soliloquies. One famous example is Hamlet's "To be or not to be, that is the question" soliloquy, in which Hamlet reveals his thoughts about life and death. Another famous example, spoken by the Shakespearean character Macbeth, follows.

Model

Is this a dagger which I see before me,
The handle toward my hand? Come, let me clutch thee.
I have thee not, and yet I see thee still.
Art thou not, fatal vision, sensible
To feeling as to sight, or art thou but
A dagger of the mind, a false creation,
Proceeding from the heat-oppressèd brain?
I see thee yet, in form as palpable
As this which now I draw.
Thou marshal'st me the way that I was going;
And such an instrument I was to use.
Mine eyes are made the fools o' th' other senses,
Or else worth all the rest. I see thee still;
And on thy blade and dudgeon gouts of blood,
Which was not so before. There's no such thing.
It is the bloody business which informs
Thus to mine eyes. Now o'er the one half-world
Nature seems dead, and wicked dreams abuse
The curtained sleep; witchcraft celebrates
Pale Hecate's offerings; and withered murder,
Alarumed by his sentinel, the wolf.
Whose howl's his watch, thus with his stealthy pace,
With Tarquin's ravishing strides, towards his design
Moves like a ghost. Thou sure and firm-set earth,
Hear not my steps, which way they walk, for fear
Thy very stones prate of my wereabout,
And take the present horror from the time,
Which now suits with it. Whiles I threat, he lives:
Words to the heat of deeds too cold breath gives.
I go, and it is done: the bell invites me.
Hear it not, Duncan, for it is a knell
That summons thee to heaven, or to hell.

The soliloquy fell out of favor with dramatists after the eighteenth century, but it never disappeared. In the twentieth century a variation of the device appeared in Eugene O'Neill's *Strange Interlude,* in which the characters speak double lines. They address one set of lines to each other, hiding the truth, and another set of lines to the AUDIENCE to reveal the truth.

someone/some one *See* ANY BODY/ANYBODY; ANY ONE/ANYONE

some/somewhat Many people use *some* when *somewhat,* meaning "slightly" or "in some degree," would be better. In FORMAL LANGUAGE use *somewhat* when the word modifies an ADJECTIVE, usually a COMPARATIVE.

> I feel <u>somewhat</u> <u>better</u>.

Otherwise, *some* is acceptable.

> High school has forced me to grow up <u>some</u>.

some time/sometime/sometimes *Some time* is an ADJECTIVE-NOUN combination referring to length of time.

> Do you have <u>some</u> <u>time</u> to help me?

Sometime means "at some indefinite time in the future."

> I'll get to my homework <u>sometime</u>.

Sometimes means "occasionally."

> <u>Sometimes</u> I can do my homework during study hall.

song As a type of literature, any LYRIC poem adapted to musical expression. Effective song lyrics are brief, relatively simple, intensely emotional.

Songs have existed since prehistoric time. They have been associated with religious ceremonies, courtship rituals, work, dancing, harvests—any event or activity that has had importance for people. Many songs tell a story and in the past were used to record and transmit historical events.

One way to classify songs is to distinguish between *folk songs* and *art songs*. Originally, folk songs were unaccompanied by instruments, or accompanied only by a simple instrument like a guitar or dulcimer. Singers usually learned folk songs by ear; they were not written down. Thus, the words (and music) could change as the songs were transmitted orally through the generations (see ORAL LITERATURE). In the distant past their composers were typically unknown.

During the Middle Ages (A.D. 500–1500) folk songs like the BALLAD told vivid, sensational stories. One of the earliest surviving ballads, dating from about 1300, was preserved along with many others in the nineteenth century in Francis J. Child's *English and Scottish Popular Ballads*. Some notable literary figures who have written ballads include John Keats, Sir Walter Scott, Samuel Taylor Coleridge, and Heinrich Heine.

Art songs, on the other hand, are more sophisticated compositions sung by more professional or accomplished singers. They are generally accompanied by instruments like the piano or an instrumental ensemble. Because they are written down, they are less susceptible to alteration. Among the earliest art songs were the *chansons* sung by French troubadours during the twelfth century. France, in fact, has produced a number of art song types, including the ballade, the rondeau, and the virelay, each of which has its own characteristics. A type of art song written in the nineteenth century by composers such as Franz Schubert, Robert Schumann, and Johannes Brahms is called the *lied.*

The songs of many modern popular songwriters have strong literary merit. The lyrics to the Beatles' song "Eleanor Rigby" are as thought-provoking as the words of any good poem. The same can be said about the lyrics of such songwriters as Peter, Paul, and Mary, the Mamas and the Papas, and Simon and Garfunkel.

sonnet A LYRIC POEM consisting of fourteen lines, following one of several RHYME SCHEMES, and usually (but not always) written in IAMBIC PENTAMETER verse.

Sonnets come in two major forms.

Italian Sonnet

The earliest sonnet form, the Italian sonnet, is sometimes referred to as the Petrarchan sonnet, after the fourteenth-century Italian poet Petrarch, who wrote a sequence of 317 such sonnets. An Italian sonnet falls into two main parts: an octave consisting of eight lines rhyming *abba abba* and a sestet consisting of six lines rhyming *cde cde,* or *cdc cdc,* or *cde dce.*

The division between the two parts of an Italian sonnet is not just one of form, though. The octave poses a problem, asks a question, expresses a doubt, or offers a reflection. The sestet is always a response to the octave, solving the problem, answering the question, resolving the doubt, or commenting on the reflection.

English Sonnet

The other major sonnet form is the English sonnet, often called the Shakespearean sonnet, in homage to Shakespeare's sequence of 154 sonnets. An English sonnet falls into into four parts: three QUATRAINS (four-line STANZAS rhyming *abab cdcd efef*) and a **couplet** (two lines rhyming *gg*). The final rhymed couplet offers a pithy wrap-up to, or comment on, the problem or emotion developed in the three quatrains.

Here is Shakespeare's Sonnet 18.

Model

> Shall I compare thee to a summer's day?
> Thou art more lovely and more temperate.
> Rough winds do shake the darling buds of May,
> And summer's lease hath all too short a date.
> Sometime too hot the eye of heaven shines,
> And often is his gold complexion dimmed;
> And every fair from fair sometime declines,
> By chance or nature's changing course untrimmed;
> But thy eternal summer shall not fade,
> Nor lose possession of that fair thou ow'st,
> Nor shall Death brag thou wand'rest in his shade,
> When in eternal lines to time thou grow'st.
> > So long as men can breathe or eyes can see,
> > So long lives this, and this gives life to thee.

Spenserian Sonnet

A third type of sonnet, written less frequently than the other two, is called the Spenserian sonnet, after the sixteenth-century British poet Edmund Spenser. The Spenserian sonnet blends the other two forms. It uses three quatrains and a final rhymed couplet, but the rhyme scheme interlocks the quatrains: *abab bcbc cdcd ee*.

Sonnets Still in Use

Although the sonnet is an old form, it continues to be widely used. Sonnet writers hone their craft through exercising the discipline and conciseness that the sonnet demands, and they enjoy the challenge to their artistry that writing a sonnet poses. Some famous earlier sonneteers include not only Shakespeare and Spenser but John Milton, William Wordsworth, Elizabeth Barrett Browning ("How do I love thee? Let me count the ways"), Dante Gabriel Rossetti, and Henry Wadsworth Longfellow. More modern poets who have written well-known sonnets include Edwin Arlington Robinson, W. H. Auden, and Edna St. Vincent Millay.

sort of/kind of/type of These are COLLOQUIALISMS that are common in everyday speech but should be avoided in FORMAL, edited language. A better option is either to use a word such as *somewhat* or to recast the sentence.

> POOR: I feel sort of sick today.
> BETTER: I feel somewhat sick today.
> POOR: George Washington was kind of reluctant to assume the presidency.
> BETTER: George Washington expressed some reluctance about becoming president.

Kind of and *type of* are acceptable when you are classifying or distinguishing.

> The ballad is one type of folk song.
> The orangutan is one kind of gorilla.

so/so that *So* is a **coordinating conjunction** that means "therefore" or "accordingly." Always use a COMMA before *so* when it introduces an INDEPENDENT CLAUSE.

The guests arrived, <u>so</u> we sat down to dinner.

So that, in contrast, is a **subordinate conjunction** that means "in order that" or "with the result that."

We added chairs <u>so that</u> we could seat eight people at the table.

Confusion arises because sometimes *so* and *so that* can be used in the same sentence with a slight change in meaning.

I'm leaving early, <u>so</u> I will arrive on time.
I'm leaving early <u>so that</u> I will arrive on time.

The first sentence states a conclusion: <u>*therefore*</u>, *I will arrive on time.* The second sentence states a reason: *I'm leaving early <u>in order to</u> arrive on time.*

sound effects (in performances) Sounds that establish a play's SETTING. Sometimes sound effects, such as a telephone ringing, are called for in a play's STAGE DIRECTIONS. You can use your imagination to think of other sounds that will help make a play's setting realistic, such as the sound of crickets chirping for a night scene.

sound effects, in poetry The use of the sound of language to set a MOOD or to reinforce the meaning of a poem. Some of the techniques poets use include ALLITERATION, ASSONANCE, CONSONANCE, ONOMATOPOEIA, RHYME, and METER.

Structural Sound Effects
The structure of a poem—including its RHYME SCHEME, FOOT, and meter—can create an effect that corresponds to the subject of the poem. In the following excerpt from "Grandfather's Clock" by Henry Clay Work, note how

the meter mimics the ticking of a clock, until the last two lines, where the meter mimics the action described:

Model

> My grandfather's clock was too large for the shelf,
>> So it stood ninety years on the floor;
> It was taller by half than the old man himself,
>> Though it weighed not a pennyweight more.
> It was bought on the morn of the day that he was born
>> And was always his treasure and pride.
> But it stopped short—never to go again—
>> When the old man died.

Effects with Word Sounds

Poets also choose words carefully to mirror what they are saying and to create a certain sound. PHONEMES have distinct sounds that create a certain mood. Poems about moving slowly or about wind blowing, for instance, often use words that repeat the long *o* sound because it mimics those actions.

One of the best examples of clever use of word sounds is Edgar Allan Poe's "The Bells." In that poem Poe describes a different kind of bell in each STANZA of the poem. Not only does he choose words that describe the bell but he also chooses words that sound like the bell being described. In the following excerpt note the repeated use of the sounds made by *t, l, s,* and *k.*

Model

> Hear the sledges with the bells—
>> Silver bells!

What a world of merriment their melody foretells!
How they tinkle, tinkle, tinkle,
   In the icy air of night!
While the stars that oversprinkle
All the heavens, seem to twinkle
   With a crystalline delight . . . .

source *See* NOTE CARD, NOTE; REFERENCE SOURCE; WORKS-
CITED LIST

Spanish, influence on English Spanish has had an enormous
influence on American English. Spanish is a ROMANCE
LANGUAGE derived from LATIN, like FRENCH and ITALIAN.

Spanish is the second most common language spoken in the United States, and, as the twenty-first century begins, some pats of the United States have heard
Spanish spoken for much longer than English. When
the frontier expanded and settlers from the English-
speaking eastern portion of the country moved west-
ward, they settled in territories originally owned by
Spain or Mexico. Towns and landmarks throughout the
West have Spanish names. *Mosquito, cigar, parade,
caramel, rodeo, stampede, mustang, ranch,* and *California*
are all Spanish words or derived from Spanish words.

In more recent times the immigration of many
Spanish-speaking people to all parts of this country has
led to the continued influence of Spanish on English.
Many words related to Spanish and Mexican foods, such
as *burrito, paella,* and *salsa* have been incorporated into
English, along with *contras, macho,* and *guerrilla.*

See also
ASIAN LANGUAGES,
INFLUENCE ON
ENGLISH
CELTIC LANGUAGES,
INFLUENCE ON
ENGLISH
FRENCH, INFLUENCE ON
ENGLISH
LATIN
and other languages

spatial order A pattern of ORGANIZATION, based on space,
used in DESCRIPTION. For example, in a SHORT STORY,
you might describe a mansion from the top down; or

See also
CHRONOLOGICAL ORDER
LOGICAL ORDER
ORDER, IMPORTANCE OF

you might describe it from a distance and then from close to the front door.

Two camera techniques, *zoom in* and *zoom out,* illustrate different ways to present a written description. When you zoom in, start by giving your reader a panoramic view of the scene. As you move closer, give a more detailed description, as in this excerpt from "The Most Dangerous Game" by Richard Connell.

Model

> [A]s he forged along he saw . . . that all the lights were in one enormous building—a lofty structure with pointed towers plunging upward into the gloom . . . . "Mirage," thought Rainsford. But it was no mirage, he found, when he opened the tall spiked iron gate. The stone steps were real enough; the massive door with a leering gargoyle for a knocker was real enough; yet about it all hung an air of unreality."

Zooming out works the opposite way. Begin with a precise, close description, then move to a wider view of the scene. Ambrose Bierce uses this technique in "An Occurrence at Owl Creek Bridge."

Model

> A man stood upon a railroad bridge . . . looking down into the swift water twenty feet below. The man's hands were behind his back, the wrists bound with a cord. A rope loosely encircled his neck. . . . At a short remove . . . was an officer in the uniform of his rank, armed. . . . [T]he railroad ran straight away

> into a forest for a hundred yards, then, curving, was lost to view. Doubtless there was an outpost farther along."

Zoom in and *zoom out* are most effective when you use them to begin or end a story.

A related type of spatial order is **order of impression.** Begin by describing the most powerful image in a scene, and then move from that illustration to less forceful images—or vice versa. For example, if you want a character's first view of a gothic mansion to inspire fear, you could describe a dreadful statue that guards the gate, and then describe other details of the mansion.

speaker, of poem In POETRY the NARRATOR of a poem is referred to as the *speaker.* As in PROSE's distinction between narrator and AUTHOR, the speaker must be distinguished from the poet. The poet, when writing a poem, adopts a PERSONA that may be nothing like the poet. The poem is written *as though* written by this persona, the speaker.

specifics Statements that apply to a particular thing, as opposed to a GENERALIZATION, which applies to more than one thing. An example of a specific statement follows.

> Our rat Lightning always steals his brother's food.

Though it may be true that dominance behavior causes all rats to either steal food or have their food stolen, the previous statement is about a *specific* rat, Lightning, and how he behaves.

A key to good writing is to balance general and specific statements. Too many generalities leave your writ-

See also
DEDUCTIVE REASONING
DETAIL
INDUCTIVE REASONING

ing vague and uninteresting, as well as factually suspect. Specific examples of general statements give depth and weight to your writing and bolster your arguments by providing factual detail.

Don't rely entirely on specifics, however. A collection of details without any overall synthesis leaves whatever point you are trying to make unstated and thus unclear to your readers.

speech *See* ORAL PRESENTATION; PERFORMANCE ASSESSMENT

See also

STYLE CHECKER

spell checker In word-processing programs a feature that checks each word in a text for spelling errors and suggests corrections.

Using Spell Checkers

Most spelling programs use the same approach: they check in text you've selected against a DICTIONARY and stop at each word not found or at double words—*the the,* for instance. When the program stops for a word not found, it displays alternative spellings. You then have a choice to make: you can instruct the program to leave the spelling as it is; you can select an alternative spelling; or you can otherwise change the spelling. Therefore *you*—not the spell checker—need to know the correct spelling of the word.

Problems with Spell Checkers

You need to read through the document yourself for errors the program cannot correct.

For instance, the program will not stop at a word that exists in a dictionary. If you typed *through* but meant *though,* the spell checker will not stop, because *through* exists in the dictionary. You can find errors with *through* only by PROOFREADING.

Spell checkers will also stop at a correctly spelled word not found in a dictionary—a proper name or an unusual word not found in a general dictionary. You must know the correct spelling of these unusual words to determine whether to change the spelling of the word.

Maximizing Spell Checkers

Most spell checkers allow you to supplement the dictionary by adding unusual words to it—words the spell checker will then recognize and accept. Use this function when you know that an unusual word will appear frequently throughout many documents. Make sure the word is spelled correctly; then select the "add" function. That word, spelled that way, will become part of the program's dictionary.

spelling *See p. 48*

spiritual SONGS sung by enslaved African Americans in the pre-Civil War South. These songs were inspired by HYMNS learned at revival meetings. Some of the spirituals reflected hope for salvation, and others were work songs sung in the fields. Some of the work songs had double meanings and were used as a form of communication among the enslaved people.

split infinitive The interruption that occurs when an ADVERB appears between *to* and the BASE FORM of a VERB.

to quickly run

(continues on p. 53)

SPELLING Few things detract from a piece of writing as much as misspelled words. Never assume that the reader doesn't know how a word is spelled or won't care whether a word is misspelled. To spell words correctly, learn the rules of spelling, memorize the exceptions, and be willing to use a dictionary.

Spelling Rules

There are many spelling rules, and they all have exceptions. While at first this can make learning the rules seem pointless, most spelling exceptions are easy enough to memorize.

ie and *ei*

You cannot tell by hearing a word whether it uses *ie* or *ei*. The general rule is that if a word has a long *e* sound, use "*i* before *e* except after *c*." So, *believe, niece, grieve,* but *conceive, receive, ceiling*. When the sound created is of a long *a*, then the spelling is also *ei*, as in *neighbor, weigh,* and *veil*. Learn the following exceptions to the general rule: *species, weird, either, neither, seize, leisure, protein, height*.

Adding Suffixes

Often, you have to change a BASE WORD somewhat before adding a SUFFIX, but these changes follow rules.

- If a base word ends in a CONSONANT followed by a *y*, change the *y* to *i* before adding the suffix, unless the suffix itself begins with *i: reply/replies, fancy/fancied, deny/deniable, fly/flying*.
- If the base word ends in a VOWEL followed by a *y*, you don't need to make any changes.

Often, you have to double the final consonant of a base word before adding a suffix.

- When the word is one SYLLABLE and ends in a *single* consonant that follows a *single* vowel, double the consonant: *shop/shopping, tip/tipped, flip/flipper.*
- When the last syllable of a base word is accented and remains accented after you add a suffix that begins with a vowel, double the consonant: *propel/propelling, regret/regrettable, occur/occurred.*
- If the base word shifts its accent, don't double the consonant: *confer/conference.*

On the question of whether or not to drop a SILENT *e,* do as follows:

- Drop the silent *e* before adding a suffix that begins with a vowel or is a *y: sizzle/sizzling, nose/nosy.* Keep the *e* if the suffix begins with a consonant: *shape/shapely.* Exceptions to this rule are base words that end in a *ce* or *ge.* When adding suffixes that begin with *a* or *o* to them, leave the *e. Change/changeable/changing.*
- When adding *ness* to a base word that ends in an *n,* keep the *n* for the base word: *sudden/suddenness.*

Adding Prefixes

Adding a PREFIX should not be much of a problem: simply add the prefix to the beginning of the base word. The only time you need to place a HYPHEN between the prefix and the base word is if the base word is a proper name (*pre-Clinton* era) or if leaving out the hyphen will confuse the reader (*re-create* is different from *recreate,* for instance).

S • 49

Words with the *seed* Sound

Words ending in the sound *seed* are almost always spelled *cede.* The only exceptions are *super<u>sede</u>, pro<u>ceed</u>, ex<u>ceed</u>, suc<u>ceed</u>.*

Finding the Correct Spelling

If you do not know how a word begins and cannot find it in the dictionary, remember some of the following spelling peculiarities:

- Words that begin with an *f* sound often begin with the letters *ph.*
- Words that begin with an *s* sound sometimes begin with the letters *ps.*
- Words that begin with a *k* sound often begin with the letters *ch.*
- Some words that begin with an *r* sound begin with the letters *rh* or *wr.*

If a dictionary gives two spellings for the same word, use the first, more common spelling.

Commonly Misspelled Words

Words easily confused with similar words are found throughout this book (for example, see AFFECT/EFFECT). Two alphabetical lists of other commonly misspelled words follow. After you've mastered the hundred words on the first list, teach yourself the second list.

100 WORDS COMMONLY MISSPELLED

accommodate	foreign	permanent
adviser	formal	physical
all right	forty	physician
analyze	fulfill	picnic
answer	giant	plural
arctic	government	popular
attendant	guarantee	potato
bruise	handle	principally
business	height	privilege
calendar	historical	psychic
candle	hospital	purpose
catastrophe	hundred	recognize
cemetery	hypocrite	relevant
choir	imagine	restaurant
climbing	incidentally	rhythm
collapse	jewelry	ridiculous
comfortable	judgment	sample
conscience	laboratory	schedule
cruise	library	sensible
curiosity	license	separate
December	lightning	solitary
definite	minuscule	somber
dependent	mischievous	sufficient
descent	mosquitoes	surgeon
desperate	muscle	theory
develop	neighbor	thorough
edible	nickel	tomato
eligible	November	traffic
embarrass	nuclear	vacuum
enormous	October	variety
familiar	original	villain
famous	pageant	Wednesday
fascinate	parallel	weight
February	pastime	

100 OTHER WORDS COMMONLY MISSPELLED

accidentally	innocent	presumption
accompaniment	interfere	probably
acknowledge	irrelevant	prophesy
adolescence	license	pursue
allegiance	luxury	quietly
anonymous	livelihood	receive
apologetically	maintenance	recommendation
arrangement	manageable	reference
benefited	maneuver	referred
boulevard	marriageable	rehearsal
bureaucrat	martyr	reminiscent
camouflage	metaphor	representative
carburetor	miniature	seize
catastrophe	misspell	sergeant
cellar	mysterious	siege
changeable	necessary	significance
discrimination	ninety	souvenir
doubt	noticeable	surprise
eighth	nuisance	susceptible
endeavor	obedience	temperature
enormous	occasionally	tomorrow
environment	occurrence	tragedy
exercise	opportunity	transcend
exhibition	orchestra	twelfth
exuberant	outrageous	unmistakable
exhaustion	pamphlet	unnatural
familiar	paralysis	unnecessary
feminine	parallel	vaccine
fundamentally	penicillin	vaudeville
grammar	permissible	vegetable
hygiene	phenomenon	vehicle
ideally	picnicking	vengeance
immediately	playwright	
indispensable	pneumonia	

(continued from p. 47)

Some teachers and books advise against splitting infinitives. They prefer

> to run quickly

However, in some cases using a split infinitive may improve the flow of your writing. Consider the following SENTENCE.

> My ambition in life is to leisurely visit every American state.

The INFINITIVE *to visit* is split by *leisurely.* Keeping the infinitive together would require placing *leisurely* before it—leisurely to visit— or after it—to visit leisurely—both of which sound awkward. Therefore, splitting the infinitive may be necessary to preserve flow and meaning.

Before splitting an infinitive, decide whether doing so will improve your writing significantly or whether your AUDIENCE will find it distracting or offensive.

spoof An humorous but gentle imitation of another work (such as a television show or an institutional memo) or of a person. A spoof differs from a PARODY or a SATIRE in that a spoof is usually intended in good fun, not to hurt someone, not to correct a behavior.

Spoof is not only a NOUN but also a VERB.

> Have you ever seen a <u>spoof</u> of *Sesame Street?*
> At my father's birthday party we <u>spoofed</u> his obsession with golf.

spoonerism A PHRASE spoken in such a way that the initial sound of one or more words is accidentally transposed, resulting in a phrase that is confusing, ludicrous, or meaningless.

INTENDED PHRASE	SPOKEN PHRASE (SPOONERISM)
hay mounds	May hounds
tons of soil	sons of toil
an oiled bicycle	a boiled icicle

The phenomenon of exchanging initial sounds is named for a man who became famous for this slip of the tongue. He was an Englishman named William Archibald Spooner (1844–1930).

square bracket *See* BRACKET

squinting modifier *See* MODIFIER; TWO-WAY MODIFIER

See also

JR.

Sr. The ABBREVIATION for the title *senior,* appearing after a person's last NAME; normally used by a man whose son has the same name. Some writers use no COMMAS in the title (John Smith Sr.), while others place a comma between the last name and the abbreviation (John Smith, Sr.). Use one but never two PERIODS after *Sr.*

stage In the theater the area on which the **play** is performed. Three general kinds of stages are used.

Proscenium Stage

The proscenium stage is the most common—and probably the oldest. The front curtain rises to show the AUDIENCE the action. The action takes place in the area that was curtained off and up to the orchestra pit (if there is one).

In a proscenium stage the parts of the stage are named from the actor's point of view. So *stage left* is to the left of the actor as he or she faces the audience. *Downstage* means toward the front of the stage—that is, toward the audience.

Thrust Stage

In this case the stage extends into the audience. In fact, theater goers may sit on three sides of the extended stage. A thrust stage, like a proscenium stage, may have a curtain, but in this case there is considerably more stage on the audience's side of the curtain.

A thrust stage is also known as an open or platform stage.

Theater-in-the-Round

Here the audience sits (often in bleacherlike seats) all the way around the playing space. Instead of a curtain going up and down, blackouts separate SCENES and ACTS. Instead of actors entering and leaving through doors or into the wings of the theater, performers use aisles, which separate sections of seats, for entrances and exits.

Theater-in-the-round is also referred to as arena stage and central stage.

stage directions Instructions, usually provided by the AUTHOR of a play, for such matters as lighting, music, scenery, the movements of actors, and the ways actors deliver the lines. Stage directions are usually included in PARENTHESES or square BRACKETS and are often printed in ITALICS.

Stage directions are a common feature in printed versions of a DRAMA, but they also occur in SCREENPLAYS for movies and in printed versions of radio plays. In Lucille Fletcher's radio play *The Hitchhiker,* for example, stage directions indicate the sounds of car wheels humming, gas being put into a car, a train, and changes in volume of "weird and shuddery" music.

The amount of detail provided in stage directions has changed over time. In the drama of the Elizabethan period, which included the plays of Shakespeare, stage directions tend to be brief, usually limited to indications that an actor was to enter or exit the stage. The one Shakespeare play that includes relatively full stage directions is *Romeo and Juliet,* but even in this play the stage directions are brief: "Enter Romeo and Mercutio, Benvolio and five or six other Maskers, torchbearers." Later in the same scene: "They march about the stage and Servingmen come forth with napkins."

Usually, though, the lines of the play itself provide "stage directions"; the AUDIENCE knows it is night, for example, not from a stage direction but because a character comes on stage carrying a lantern. (When you are reading a play by Shakespeare, remember that no manuscripts in Shakespeare's hand survive, so we don't know whether he provided any stage directions at all or whether someone else added stage directions later.)

Twentieth-century writers, in contrast, provide more stage directions. For many playwrights a play is not just a SCRIPT for actors. They see both the DIALOGUE and the stage directions as working together to make up the total work. The best example might be the American playwright Eugene O'Neill, who provides lengthy and elaborate stage directions. They sometimes go on for several paragraphs. The result is that reading a play by O'Neill is somewhat like reading a NOVEL.

standard English The primary variety of English accepted by academic institutions, professions, the national media, and so on. Standard English is usually spoken by the people who hold the most influence over these areas of society, and standard English changes slowly.

Characteristics of standard English show up in all aspects of written and spoken language, including GRAMMAR AND USAGE, VOCABULARY, SPELLING, PUNCTUATION, and even PRONUNCIATION. Following are a few examples of standard versus nonstandard English words and expressions.

See also
COLLOQUIALISM
DIALECT
FORMAL LANGUAGE
INFORMAL LANGUAGE
JARGON
SLANG

Grammar and Usage

IRREGULAR VERB forms sometimes present difficulties.

STANDARD: I have swum in that pool before.
NONSTANDARD: I have swam in that pool before.
STANDARD: If Barry had gone earlier, he would have caught that plane.
NONSTANDARD: If Barry had went earlier, he would have caught that plane.
STANDARD: Sue lay down for a nap.
NONSTANDARD: Sue laid down for a nap.

Vocabulary, Spelling

Sometimes English users confuse words because of their similar sounds (see HOMOGRAPH, HOMONYM, HOMOPHONE).

STANDARD: Angela would have mowed the lawn if it hadn't rained.
NONSTANDARD: Angela would of mowed the lawn if it hadn't rained.

Punctuation

Rules for punctuation sometimes seem arbitrary and tedious, but they, too, are part of standard English.

STANDARD: Debra was visiting her mother. She saw her sister, too.

NONSTANDARD: Debra was visiting her mother, she saw her sister, too.

STANDARD: Jake asked, "What would you like to eat?"

NONSTANDARD: Jake asked, "What would you like to eat?".

standardized test A general-knowledge test that measures knowledge and aptitude and is taken by many people throughout the country, whose average scores are used as a standard by which each person's performance is measured.

College admission tests, such as the SAT or ACT, are standardized tests that measure a variety of different learning skills; other tests measure knowledge of a specific subject area; and some tests are designed to measure abilities such as career aptitudes.

Standardized tests are primarily, if not completely, **objective**; that is, they consist of multiple-choice or other kinds of SHORT-ANSWER QUESTIONS. Some college admission tests include an ESSAY portion, however.

Taking Standardized Tests

When taking a standardized test, read each question carefully so that it is clear what is being asked; read each answer choice carefully. Never choose an answer until you have read all the choices.

Standardized tests usually include reading comprehension questions, in which you are given a passage to read and then must answer questions about the material. Read the material completely before answering the questions, although you may find it helpful to SKIM the

questions first to set a purpose for your reading (see SET-
TING A PURPOSE FOR READING).

When answering ANALOGIES and sentence comple-
tion and spatial relations questions, you need to identify
the relationship between the items in the question
before you can find the correct answer.

Do not get stuck on one question for too long; allow
yourself an approximate amount of time per question
(based on the total time available and the number of
questions). If you exceed that time, place a small mark
next to the question so that you can return to it, and
move on. Not only will you answer more questions, but
you will keep momentum and confidence; falling
behind increases the pressure and unnecessarily creates
tension.

Before taking any standardized test, think about
eliminating any distractions within your control so that
you will be able to focus on the questions. Get plenty of
sleep, eat well, arrive early, bring extra pencils, a watch,
and tissues—such planning will help eliminate many
distractions and allow you to be more relaxed.

Also find out if it is to your advantage to skip or
guess the answer to questions.

standards Minimum expected levels of knowledge for students or teachers. These minimums may be set by state
or local governments or departments of education. Standards are sometimes referred to as minimum competen-
cy levels.

Standards may also describe the general goals of a
particular field of study. For instance, the National
Council of Teachers of English (NCTE) outlines several
standards that define the various goals of the study of
language arts. One example of these standards follows:

Model

> Students read a wide range of literature from many periods in many genres to build an understanding of the many dimensions (e.g., philosophical, ethical, aesthetic) of human experience.

stanza The basic unit of a work of VERSE, or POETRY. Except for FREE VERSE, the basic unit contains a METER and RHYME SCHEME that appear throughout the work. The stanzas act as divisions of the poem.

A stanza can be as short as two lines, known as a couplet. A QUATRAIN, another type of stanza, contains four lines.

See also
LITERATURE,
    INTERPRETING

stated theme A direct statement of a work's meaning by the AUTHOR of the literary work. In the statement the author expresses the work's central idea rather than leaving it up to the reader to determine.

Most literary works have an IMPLIED THEME; the reader himself or herself interprets the central idea, or point, of the story. Different readers may see different themes in a given work.

Stated themes are more common in fairy tales or FABLES, which actually announce "the moral of the story."

See also
DYNAMIC CHARACTER

static character In a work of FICTION or DRAMA, a CHARACTER who undergoes little or no change during the course of the story. Static characters are often, though not necessarily, MINOR CHARACTERS. Usually, the MAIN CHARACTERS in a story grow—or sometimes deteriorate—during the story's action, and this change contributes to the

PLOT. But static characters stay relatively the same throughout the story; at the story's end they are no different from the way they were at the beginning. Lack of change in a character often leads critics to give a work a negative REVIEW.

stationary/stationery   *Stationary* means "not moving."

> I exercise on a <u>stationary</u> bike.

Stationery means "writing paper."

> I use engraved <u>stationery</u> for writing letters.

> ## Memory Jogger
> The only vowel in *letter* is *e*, so use *station**e**ry* to write letters.

stereotype   An oversimplified judgment of a person, issue, race of people, and so on. Stereotypes often reflect prejudices that have been handed down based on misunderstandings, half-truths, or other inaccuracies.

   Women like children better than men do and *Football players are strong but shallow* are stereotypes. Stereotypical thinking can cause you to draw damaging conclusions. Extreme stereotypes can lead to racism, bigotry, religious persecution, and other forms of intolerance.

   Stereotyping can alienate a listener from a speaker or a reader from a writer. Check your writing to be sure you don't use stereotypes about gender, health and physical ability, religion, race, or sexual orientation. Gender stereotypes, in particular, are so pervasive that it is easy for them to go unnoticed. But not all girls are concerned about their appearance, and not all boys are insensitive.

   If you are writing about a someone who happens to have a disability or illness, consider whether the disability or illness is relevant to your discussion. If not, don't mention it. If it is relevant, pay attention to how you present the topic. The phrase *a woman with breast*

See also
CONNOTATION
EUPHEMISM
LOADED WORD
OVERGENERALIZATION
REASONING

cancer is preferable to *a victim of breast cancer.* The preferred phrasing gives the subject more control over the situation: she controls it; it doesn't control her.

Religious stereotypes abound because different religions present various and often competing worldviews.

Racial and ethnic stereotypes have historically led to oppression or eradication of large numbers of people. Hitler's persecution of Jews in World War II, the systematic submergence of Native American cultures, and slavery in the United States occurred because of racial stereotyping.

Stereotyping sexual orientation—claiming, for example, *everyone at school is attracted to the opposite sex*—is just beginning to get widespread attention. As with any other labeling, use sexual-orientation information only if it is relevant to your discussion.

stet A term used by a printer, proofreader, or editor to indicate that a character, word, or line marked for omission should stand—that is, should not be taken out after all. The term comes from a form of the LATIN word *stare,* which means "to stand." At times an editor or proofreader may supplement or replace the written order *stet* with a series of dots below the crossed-out material. For example, the person who marked up the next line

stet
William ~~Archibald~~ Spooner, ~~1844–1930~~

wants the final text to read as follows:

William Archibald Spooner

stock character *See* FLAT CHARACTER

story *See* NARRATIVE; SHORT STORY; STORYTELLING, ORAL

story plan (story map) A tool for considering story elements
before beginning to DRAFT a NARRATIVE. You can generate a story plan by clustering or using an OUTLINE or
TABLE. The story plan should address questions about
each element, as the following list suggests.
plot:

- PLOT: What is the story's central problem or conflict?
What roadblocks will the character(s) face while
attempting to solve the problem? How will the prob-
lem be solved?
- CHARACTERS: Who are the characters in the story?
Which characters need to be fully developed? How
will you present them to your AUDIENCE: through
appearance, action, DIALOGUE, MONOLOGUE?
- SETTING: How important is setting to your story?
What elements of setting do you want to include (for
example, weather, location, time period)?
- POINT OF VIEW: Which point of view will you use
(FIRST PERSON, OMNISCIENT, limited THIRD PERSON,
objective)? Why will you use this point of view?
- THEME: What is the theme, or GENERALIZATION about
life, in your story? Do you want to state it clearly or
imply it?

storytelling, oral The act of READING or telling a story to a
live AUDIENCE.
    Before the existence of printed books, storytellers
occupied a prominent place in the cultures in which
they lived. Storytellers gathered and stored the collective
memory and wisdom of the group. In recounting stories
about the origins of the world (see MYTH) or the heroic

deeds of the group's ancestors, they not only entertained and instructed their listeners but gave the group an identity that persisted from generation to generation.

While the development of the printed book (as well as movies and television) may have lessened the prominence of the storyteller, the art of oral storytelling has by no means disappeared. Listeners today respond to the performances of a good storyteller with perhaps as much enjoyment as their ancestors did many hundreds of years ago. Oral storytelling today can be as simple as a parent making up and telling a bedtime story or a librarian reading to a group of children on a Saturday morning. Oral storytelling can also be as elaborate as the reading, usually by a number of readers taking turns over twenty-four hours, of James Joyce's famous novel *Ulysses*.

Strictly speaking, reading from a text is called ORAL INTERPRETATION. Oral storytelling, in contrast, usually implies recounting a story without a written text. The story can be a favorite story that has survived through generations of oral storytelling. Or the story may be the storyteller's own creation.

Again, this type of oral storytelling can be as simple as telling a good joke—one that develops a story and leads the listener on a delightful journey to the punch line—or as elaborate as the annual festivals at which storytellers from throughout the country assemble to share performances with audiences.

If you are in a position to tell a story orally, see the checklist at left for some tips to follow to increase your chances of success.

> ## Checklist
>
> ORAL STORYTELLING
>
> 1. If you choose a story you like, you can convey that enthusiasm to your listeners.
> 2. Know the story well, but do not memorize it. Your goal is to *tell* the story, not *recite* it.
> 3. Use vivid language that will help your listeners *see* the action and the characters.
> 4. Practice, practice, practice.

stream of consciousness A writing STYLE that mimics the natural, often random, flow of a CHARACTER's thoughts and mental images. This style is characterized by RUN-ON sentences and an absence of COHERENCE or logical pattern. Familiar examples of this style include Ernest Hemingway's story "The Snows of Kilimanjaro," Katherine Anne Porter's "The Jilting of Granny Weatherall," and one of the earliest and best-known examples, James Joyce's *Ulysses*.

stress *See* ACCENT (STRESS)

stringy sentence A long SENTENCE that runs a series of ideas together with *and's,* creating a sentence in which no particular idea stands out.

> STRINGY SENTENCE: There is high fire danger this August in the western United States, and this danger is causing concern, and the fire crews are recruiting additional volunteers to meet the projected firefighting needs.

You can correct a stringy sentence in several ways. You can choose more precise CONJUNCTIONS to link your ideas; you can subordinate some ideas to others (see SUBORDINATION); or you can break up the sentence.

> IMPROVED WITH CONJUNCTIVE ADVERB: The high fire danger this August in the western United States is causing concern; consequently, fire crews are recruiting additional volunteers to meet the projected firefighting needs.
>
> IMPROVED BY DIVIDING SENTENCE: The high fire danger this August in the western United States is causing concern. Fire crews are recruiting additional volunteers to meet the projected firefighting needs.

See also
SENTENCE COMBINING

structural clues The parts of a word—its PREFIX, SUFFIX, and ROOT—that help you figure out the word's meaning. Most prefixes and suffixes have specific meanings, and knowing these, along with recognizing roots, can help you figure out the meaning of unfamiliar words.

For example, the prefix *poly* means "many," the prefix *hydr* means "water," the suffix *phobia* means "fear," and the suffix *iatric* means "relating to medical treatment." *Hydrophobia* means "fear of the water," and *hydriatric* means "water treatment or therapy."

You can "translate" roots by thinking of familiar words that are similar. For instance, you may not know the word *polyphonic,* but you recognize *phonic* from *phonics, phone,* and *phonograph,* all of which have to do with sound. So *polyphonic* has something to do with "many sounds."

See also

ACTIVE READING
DIALOGUE WITH TEXT

study skills Specific strategies that, whether used consciously or unconsciously, will make your study time more effective and efficient. Students who consistently do well may not necessarily be smarter, luckier, or even harder working than students who struggle. Their success may result from working smart.

1. **Take Good Notes in Class.** Don't just jot down words and phrases in a list. Try to organize your notes in an OUTLINE—either during class or later. Pay attention to cues your teacher gives you about what information is most important: hand gestures, tone of voice, words such as "most important," writing on the board.

2. **Organize Your Study Time.** Pick a spot where you're comfortable. Eliminate distractions. Set goals. Break longer assignments down into parts.

Switch to a different subject after thirty minutes or an hour to keep your mind fresh.

3. **Figure Out How you Best Learn.** Is it by writing a SUMMARY? By outlining? By making CHARTS, TABLES, or GRAPHS? By reading aloud? By discussing issues with others?

4. **Practice Your Reading Skills.** Remember that there are three types of reading: SKIMMING, which is glancing over the text to get a sense of its structure and main ideas; SCANNING, which is reading rapidly to locate specific information; and in-depth reading, which involves detailed attention to the text.

5. **Use the SQ3R Method.** It's a study method by which you *survey* the material by skimming, think of *questions* you have about the topic, *read* the material in depth, *record* notes and answers to your questions, and *review* your answers, checking them against the text.

6. **Use Mnemonic Devices.** A MNEMONIC device is any handy way to memorize information, especially information that is easily confused. Common examples include the SPELLING rule "Use *i* before *e* except after *c*" and "<u>M</u>y <u>v</u>ery <u>e</u>xcellent <u>m</u>other <u>j</u>ust <u>s</u>erved <u>us</u> <u>n</u>ine <u>p</u>ickles" (to remember the order of the planets in the solar system: Mercury, Venus, Earth, Mars, Jupiter, Saturn, Uranus, Neptune, and Pluto).

style *See p. 68*

style checker Also called a *grammar checker* or a *text analyzer,* a word-processing tool to help you revise your writing

(continues on p. 72)

STYLE In the context of language study, the way in which something is written; the distinctive features that characterize a way of writing.

People who read a lot can distinguish some writers from other writers by their writing styles. To underscore this point, this entry will examine passages of PROSE writing in English from different centuries—by Ernest Hemingway from the twentieth century and by Jane Austen from the eighteenth.

Experienced readers know that Ernest Hemingway's style is marked by mostly simple words and mostly straightword **simple sentences** of about equal length. Here is an excerpt from Hemingway's short story "A Day's Wait."

Model

> Downstairs, the doctor left three different medicines in different colored capsules with instructions for giving them. One was to bring down the fever, another a purgative, the third to overcome an acid condition. The germs of influenza can only exist in an acid condition, he explained. He seemed to know all about influenza and said there was nothing to worry about if the fever did not ago above one hundred and four degrees. This was a light epidemic of flu and there was no danger if you avoided pneumonia.

Here, now, is an excerpt from the NOVEL *Pride and Prejudice* by Jane Austen. It's full of **complex sentences,** sentences of different lengths, PARALLELISM, sophisticated VOCABULARY, and many MODIFIERS—both single words and PHRASES.

Model

> When the ladies removed after dinner, Elizabeth ran up to her sister, and seeing her well guarded from cold, attended her into the drawing-room; where she was welcomed by her two friends with many professions of pleasure; and Elizabeth had never seen them so agreeable as they were during the hour which passed before the gentlemen appeared. Their powers of conversation were considerable. They could describe an entertainment with accuracy, relate an anecdote with humour, and laugh at their acquaintance with spirit.

Jane Austen's writing has a markedly different style from Ernest Hemingway's. The difference might be expected since the two passages are from different centuries. Even within the same time period, however, writers can have distinct styles.

In contrast to the lean style of Hemingway stands the more elaborate writing of William Faulkner, who lived and died almost simultaneously with Hemingway. Here is an excerpt from the short story "A Rose for Emily" by Faulkner. Note the descriptions within descriptions within descriptions.

Model

> When Miss Emily Grierson died, our whole town went to her funeral: the men through a sort of respectful affection for a fallen monument, the women mostly out of curiosity to see the inside of her house, which no one save an old manservant—a combined gardener and cook—had seen in at least ten years.

It was a big, squarish frame house that had once been white, decorated with cupolas and spires and scrolled balconies in the heavily lightsome style of the seventies, set on what had once been our most select street. But garages and cotton gins had encroached and obliterated even the august names of that neighborhood; only Miss Emily's house was left, lifting its stubborn and coquettish decay above the cotton wagons and the gasoline pumps—an eyesore among eyesores. . . .

In addition to sentence length and complexity, SYN-TAX, and DICTION, writing styles stand out from one another on the basis of FIGURATIVE LANGUAGE and IMAGERY. Both Hemingway and Faulkner won the NOBEL PRIZE FOR LITERATURE, and both of them gave acceptance speeches. First, read Hemingway's words about what a writer does. As in his FICTION, here Hemingway is again straightforward. He comes close to creating a METAPHOR in the final sentence . . . but doesn't quite.

Model

For a true writer each book should be a new beginning where he tries again for something that is beyond attainment. He should always try for something that has never been done or that others have tried and failed. Then sometimes, with great luck, he

> will succeed. How simple the writing of literature would be if it were only necessary to write in another way what has been well written. It is because we have had such great writers in the past that a writer is driven far out past where he can go, out to where no one can help him.

Now read Faulkner's words about what a writer does, and note the metaphor with which he ends his speech.

Model

> I believe that man will not merely endure: he will prevail. He is immortal, not because he alone among creatures has an inexhaustible voice, but because he has a soul, a spirit capable of compassion and sacrifice and endurance. The poets', the writer's, duty is to write about these things. It is his privilege to help man endure by lifting his heart, by reminding him of the courage and honor and hope and pride and compassion and pity and sacrifice which have been the glory of his past. The poet's voice need not merely be the record of man, it can be one of the props, the pillars to help him endure and prevail.

When comparing styles across centuries or between two contemporaries, it is not necessary to judge one style as better than the other. But it is important to be aware of the many choices writers make—in every sentence, in every piece of DIALOGUE, in every PARAGRAPH—to create their own sound, their own style.

(continued from p. 67)

Helpful Hint

Checking Your Checker

When using a style checker, don't be afraid to check its advice against another source, such as a textbook or this encyclopedia.

---

by calling attention to possible ERRORS. Unfortunately, because many writing mistakes don't fall into mathematically precise categories, all style checkers miss mistakes but flag some correct usages as mistakes. Just as a SPELL CHECKER will not solve all your spelling problems, neither will a style checker solve all your sentence-level problems.

Commonly used style checkers will alert you relatively well to WORDINESS, inflated language or SLANG, and PASSIVE VOICE. They are not so good at flagging sentence FRAGMENTS or RUN-ONS. They do not notice many examples of faulty PARALLELISM, MISPLACED MODIFIERS, or DANGLING MODIFIERS, AWKWARD WRITING, missing words, and unnecessary SHIFTS in POINT OF VIEW or TENSE.

subject complement A NOUN or ADJECTIVE that comes after a form of BE or another LINKING VERB and names or describes the SUBJECT. If the complement is an adjective or ADJECTIVE PHRASE, it is called a PREDICATE ADJECTIVE. If it is a noun or NOUN PHRASE, it is called a PREDICATE NOUN or predicate nominative.

PREDICATE NOUN
Jason was the <u>president</u> of his class.

PREDICATE ADJECTIVE
Jenny appeared <u>tired and cranky</u>.

subjective case *See* CASE, NOMINATIVE

subjective writing Writing that clearly expresses an OPINION. EDITORIALS in a newspaper or magazine, opinion or advice columns, and book and film REVIEWS are all examples of subjective writing. As a reader you must always be aware that subjective writing states one's personal opinion, not necessarily FACT.

Subjective writing, as opposed to OBJECTIVE WRITING, is usually INFORMAL and uses the FIRST PERSON or SECOND PERSON; objective writing tends to range from semiformal to FORMAL and commonly uses the THIRD PERSON.

subject (of sentence) The word or PHRASE that performs the action in the SENTENCE; the word or phrase about which something is being said. A variety of words and phrases can act as subjects of a sentence.

> My brother is ten years old.
>
>   [subject: *My brother*, NOUN]
>
> They are visiting from Illinois.
>
>   [subject: *They*, PRONOUN]
>
> In summer swimming is one of my favorite forms of exercise.
>
>   [subject: *swimming*, GERUND]
>
> Whether we arrive on time will depend on traffic.
>
>   [subject: *Whether we arrive on time*, NOUN CLAUSE.]

Sometimes, determining the subject of a sentence is difficult. Use the checklist to help with hard-to-find subjects.

In the example in the checklist, the subject is *a rabbit.* This is the **complete subject,** or the group of words acting as the subject. The SIMPLE SUBJECT, the main or most important part of the complete subject, is *rabbit.*

Agreement with Verb

Subjects may be SINGULAR or PLURAL. The NUMBER of the verb must match the number of the subject when

---

Checklist

FINDING SUBJECTS

1. Find all the PREPOSITIONAL PHRASES in the sentence, and cross them out. The subject is never in a prepositional phrase.
2. Find the VERBS in the sentence.
3. Ask who or what is doing the action of the verbs. One of your answers will usually be the subject.

Example:
In the yard a rabbit dug a hole.
FIRST: Cross out prepositional phrase—*in the yard*
SECOND: Find the verb—*dug*
THIRD: Ask who/what did the digging—*a rabbit*
SUBJECT OF THE SENTENCE: *a rabbit*

---

you're using the PRESENT TENSE (see AGREEMENT, SUBJECT-VERB).

> Trees outside my window block the sun.
> > [plural subject and verb]
>
> A tree outside my window blocks the sun.
> > [singular subject and verb]

Sometimes a sentence has a compound subject, two or more subjects that often—but not always—take a plural verb.

> Chicken and fish have different flavors.
> > [subject: chicken and fish]

Placement in the Sentence

In a DECLARATIVE SENTENCE the subject usually precedes the PREDICATE. However, in some sentences the predicate or part of the predicate comes before the subject. Such sentences are called INVERTED SENTENCES.

> Gone is the queen. [The subject, *queen,* comes after the verb.]

INTERROGATIVE SENTENCES place the subject after part of the predicate.

> Have you see my pen? [*Have,* part of the predicate, precedes *you,* the subject.]

subject (of writing) *See* PREWRITING

See also

IMPERATIVE MOOD
INDICATIVE MOOD
MOOD
VERB TENSE

subjunctive mood The form of a VERB that expresses a condition contrary to fact, an idea in doubt or question, or a wish. In some cases the subjunctive stands out by sounding FORMAL.

One of the most frequently uttered subjunctive expressions is *If I were. . .*(see IF I WAS/IF I WERE). *Were* is in the subjunctive mood because the statement is contrary to fact or is a wish.

Some phrases such as *recommend that. . .* and *insist that. . .* lead into the subjunctive because they indicate an idea in doubt or question:

> I recommend that he <u>see</u> me first.

There is a question of whether he will see me (I'm only recommending it), so the verb *see* is in the subjunctive mood.

In the next case the speaker expresses a wish:

> He wishes he <u>were</u> closer to the beach.

Present Subjunctive and Past Subjunctive

The present subjunctive uses the BASE FORM OF THE VERB.

> I recommend that you <u>be</u> present.

The past subjunctive is the same as the PAST TENSE except for *be;* the past subjunctive of *be* is *were.*

> If I <u>studied</u> harder, I would have passed.
> If I <u>were</u> more studious, I would have passed.

subordinate clause *See* CLAUSE; DEPENDENT CLAUSE; SENTENCE

subordinate conjunction *See* CONJUNCTION; GRAMMAR AND USAGE; SO/SO THAT

subordination Placing words, PHRASES, or CLAUSES in a secondary position in a SENTENCE to make the main point more distinct. A sentence element that is subordinate

See also

COORDINATION
DEPENDENT CLAUSE
SENTENCE COMBINING

cannot stand alone; it depends on the rest of the sentence. Subordination adds to sentence variety.

> NO SUBORDINATION: The conditions at Valley Forge were harsh, but General Washington stayed on there with his troops.
>
> SUBORDINATION: Although the conditions at Valley Forge were harsh, General Washington stayed on with his troops.
>
> General Washington stayed on with his troops, although conditions at Valley Forge were harsh.

subplot In a literary work a minor story that has its own RISING and FALLING ACTION but is not as detailed as the main PLOT. Often the subplot's CONFLICT parallels that of the main plot; the conflict can be an additional source of tension for a story's MAIN CHARACTERS, or it can involve MINOR CHARACTERS.

See also

SUPERSCRIPT

subscript A character or SYMBOL written beneath and slightly to one side of a letter or number. The word *example* below is followed by a subscript numeral.

$$example_2$$

You may see subscripts in mathematics or science texts.

subtitle *See* CAPITALIZATION; TITLE

suffix A MORPHEME or SYLLABLE added to a ROOT or BASE WORD to create a new word with a different, but related meaning. In addition to suffixes that denote NOUN PLURALS, SINGULAR VERBS, TENSES, or COMPARATIVE or SUPERLATIVE forms, many suffixes can change a word from one PART OF SPEECH to another. (Some books place a HYPHEN in front of letters to signify a suffix: for example, *-ant* and *-dom*.)

Noun-Forming Suffixes

Some suffixes create NOUNS. Here are examples.

Suffix	Examples	Meaning of Suffix
ant, ent	occupant dependent	"one who does an action"
dom	kingdom freedom	"state" or "condition"
ness	kindness friendliness	"quality" or "state"
ment	judgment treatment	concrete result," "action," or "process"
ence ance	reference preference performance	"action," "process," "quality," or "state"

Additionally, the suffix *age* changes one noun into another noun, as in *mile + age = mileage*.

Adjective-Forming Suffixes

Examples of suffixes that change a root or base word into an ADJECTIVE follow.

Suffix	Examples	Meaning of Suffix
ful	hopeful fearful	"full of"
less	hopeless fearless	"without"
ous	joyous	"full of"
ish	boyish kittenish	"acting like"
able ible	breakable contemptible	"capable of " or "tending to"

Verb-Forming Suffixes

Some suffixes, such as the following, change a word into a VERB.

Suffix	Examples	Meaning of Suffix
en	quicken shorten	"to become" or "to make"
ize	crystallize maximize	"to become" or "to make"

Spelling

Here are some tips that will help you with SPELLING when you add suffixes to words.

1. When you add a suffix that begins with a CONSONANT to a root that ends with a SILENT E, keep the e: *placement, rarely.* Exceptions are *awful, acknowledgment,* and *judgment.* Drop the silent *e,* however, if the suffix begins with a VOWEL or *y: excitable, shiny.*

   If the suffix begins with an *a* or *o* and the root ends with *ce* or *ge,* keep the *e: changeable, traceable.*

2. When you add a suffix to a word that ends in a consonant + *y,* change the *y* to an *i* unless the suffix begins with an *i: try + ed = tried,* but *copy + ing = copying.*

See also

PARAPHRASE

summary A shortened and rewritten version of important material from an original **composition.** A summary is one of four ways you can take NOTES for RESEARCH PAPERS, reports, speeches, and other kinds of writing. Other types of note-taking include paraphrasing, quoting, and recording personal comments.

When you write a summary, consider the PURPOSE for the piece you are writing; focus on the material you need when you condense the information. You may include QUOTATIONS from the original material if you need to, but remember to use QUOTATION MARKS around the material, and cite the SOURCE in your composition.

To summarize, condense information from a chapter to a page, a page to a PARAGRAPH, or a paragraph to a SENTENCE. See, for example, the original passage and summary below. In this instance, the paragraph is condensed to one sentence.

Original Passage

The word *utopia* was coined in 1516, when Sir Thomas More published a fictional work describing a perfect society, New Utopia. Utopian literature is often written during times of social upheaval; many utopian works were written in the nineteenth century, as western societies transformed from agricultural to industrial cultures. Dystopian novels, or novels that describe a society gone awry, arose in the twentieth century as a challenge to these ideal societies. Instead of seeing increasing industry and technology as the promise of a better life for mankind (and womankind), dystopian novels often see these advances as means for individual and cultural exploitation and control.

Summary

Utopian literature—describing perfect societies—was popular in the nineteenth century as an optimistic response to technological development; dystopian literature—describing societies in decline—arose in the twentieth century and sees industry and technology as means to control society.

See also

COMPARATIVE DEGREE

COMPARISON OF
  MODIFIERS

─ Helpful Hint ─

Creating Superlatives

One syllable? Use *est*: *fastest, loudest, slowest*.

Two syllables ending in *y?* Use *est*: *prettiest*.

Two syllables not ending in *y?* Use *most*: *most honest*.

Three or more syllables? Use *most*: *most diligent, most beautiful*.

superlative degree Form of a MODIFIER used to compare more than two entities. The superlative form tells which entity exhibits the greatest amount of a trait. Usually the superlative is formed by adding the SUFFIX *est* to an ADJECTIVE or ADVERB or by inserting *most* before it.

Some adjectives and adverbs require IRREGULAR COMPARISON. Use the chart below as a reference.

Adjective/Adverb	Superlative
good, well	best
bad, ill	worst
many, much	most
less	least

superscript A character or SYMBOL written above and slightly to one side of a letter or number. Superscripts refer readers to another location in a text, such as a FOOTNOTE, **endnote,** or content note (see DOCUMENTATION). Superscripts are common in math: 10^2, 10^n. The word *example* at the end of this sentence is followed by a superscript numeral: *example*[2].

See also

USE TO/USED TO

suppose to **Nonstandard** form of the expression *supposed to,* meaning "to expect" or "to obligate." Don't overlook the *d*.

You were <u>supposed to</u> be home by nine.

sure, surely Do not use *sure* when you need an ADVERB or INTENSIFIER.

See also

REAL / VERY / REALLY

> NOT You sure know your way around the library.
> BUT You surely know your way around the library.

If *surely* sounds stilted to you, try a SYNONYM.

> You <u>certainly</u> know your way around the library.
> <u>Without a doubt,</u> you know your way around the library.

surprise ending The DÉNOUEMENT, usually of a work of FICTION or DRAMA, that comes as a surprise to the reader (and perhaps to some of the CHARACTERS as well) but is consistent with the thread of the story.

Much fiction depends on surprise endings. Murder MYSTERIES, such as those written by Agatha Christie, rely for their effect on the surprising exposure of the criminal at the end.

The term *surprise ending,* though, has been most closely associated with the American writer O. Henry. An often-cited example of O. Henry's use of the surprise ending is "The Gift of the Magi." In this SHORT STORY a husband wants to buy a set of combs as a Christmas present for his wife, who has beautiful long hair. At the same time, the wife wants to buy her husband a chain to match his pocket watch. In the surprise ending the husband learns that to raise money for the chain, his wife has sold her long hair—and the wife learns that to raise money for the combs, her husband has sold his watch.

survey A research technique used while gathering information for a RESEARCH PAPER or in preparing a MULTIMEDIA PRESENTATION.

In conducting a survey, you question a sample of people to get their views on the topic you are researching. You might question respondents orally or in writing. The goal is to get a sense of what a range of people think about an issue. If you were researching, for example, the topic of preventing violence in schools, you might question students, teachers, school administrators, parents, and law-enforcement people.

Here are some tips on developing a good survey.

1. Survey as wide a range of people as you can, given the constraints on your time and their availability.
2. Develop survey questions that prompt specific, measurable responses. Don't ask "What should be done to prevent school violence?" That's too vague. A better, more specific question might be, "Do you support random locker searches in schools?"
3. Make your questions as neutral as possible. Avoid questions that seem to invite a certain response.

suspense The anticipation readers or an AUDIENCE feel about the outcome of a NOVEL, SHORT STORY, DRAMA, or movie.

Nearly all literature that tells a story relies on suspense. Suspense is critical in some types of FICTION, such as the murder MYSTERY or spy thriller. In others suspense may be more subdued, yet the reader still feels a building sense of anticipation about the fate of the CHARACTERS.

Suspense can present two different puzzles. In one the reader is uncertain about who, what, or how. In a murder mystery, for example, the reader is usually uncertain about who committed the crime and how he or she pulled it off. With the other suspense puzzle, the reader knows what is going to happen but is uncertain about when. In the movie *Jaws,* for example, the viewer knows that the shark is going to attack but is uncertain about when.

suspension of disbelief *See* FICTION

syllabication The process of dividing a word into its SYLLA-BLES. The word *syllabication,* for instance, consists of five syllables: *syl-lab-i-ca-tion.*

Ordinarily a syllable must contain one, and only one, VOWEL sound; some syllables, such as the *i* above, can consist of only a vowel. Many syllables, though, consist of the vowel and one or more CONSONANT sounds. A word's syllabication corresponds to natural groupings of consonants and a vowel in the word's pronunciation.

Syllabication (sometimes called *syllabification*) serves two purposes. One is as a guide to the pronunciation of the word. The other is to show how to divide a word at the end of a line in printed or typewritten text. In the example given above, a writer or typist knows that the word can be divided in this way—*syllabi-cation*—but not in this way—*syllabic-ation.*

syllable In spoken language a unit of uninterrupted sound. Teachers often demonstrate the syllabic content of a word by clapping to the beat of the word. For example, *the* contains just one unit or syllable; *demonstrate* contains three: *de·mon·strate.*

If you must hyphenate a word at the end of a line (see HYPHEN), do so only between syllables.

syllogism In DEDUCTIVE REASONING a set of statements from which a conclusion logically follows. It consists of a major **premise** (*All teachers at this school are college graduates*), minor premise (*Mr. Powers is a teacher at this school*), and a conclusion that follows from the premises (*Mr. Powers is a college graduate*).

symbol The term *symbol* is used in two primary ways. One is to refer to typographic symbols. Thus, the ampersand (&) is a symbol that denotes the word *and.* The letters of the alphabet are all symbols that stand for sounds, which in turn are symbols for objects and ideas.

As a literary device *symbol* is somewhat harder to define. A symbol is any object (or something such as a color) that stands for more than itself; it carries with it a set of meanings and associations that shed light on the work's THEME, SETTING, or CHARACTERIZATION.

An effective symbol works both literally and as FIGURATIVE LANGUAGE. In Charles Dickens's *A Tale of Two Cities,* for example, the Bastille, a prison in Paris, is both an actual prison, serving as the site of some of the NOVEL's action, and a symbol for the oppression of the French people. In Thomas Hardy's *The Return of the Native* the blindness of the main character, Clym, is not only a literal blindness that plays a part in the story's PLOT but is also symbolic of his inability to see the true nature of his relationship with his wife, Eustacia.

Some symbols are universal; that is, they have automatic associations independent of the author's use of them. Red, for example, tends to suggest passion, while a voyage—such as the ocean voyage in Herman

Melville's *Moby Dick* or the trip down the Mississippi River in Mark Twain's *Huckleberry Finn*—suggests the passage of a human community through space and time. AUTHORS frequently count on readers' recognizing these universal associations.

Other symbols take on meaning only through the author's specific use of them. In *A Farewell to Arms* Ernest Hemingway uses rain, which can otherwise have life-giving properties, to symbolize death as the novel proceeds.

Symbolism should be distinguished from an IMAGERY. While the meanings of the two terms overlap, an image is a word that evokes a sensory impression. Thus, an author might use imagery that suggests "tree." That image, though, is not a symbol, though it might become symbolic if the author uses *tree* to suggest a meaning beyond itself.

symposium A word, derived from GREEK, meaning "drinking together," referring to a banquet.

Early Greek banquets were frequently the scene of spirited discussions. By extension the term *symposium* came to refer to a discussion by several persons of a single topic, then to a collection of speeches or even written ESSAYS. One of the most famous dialogues written by the Greek philosopher Plato is called *The Symposium*.

In the United States the early Transcendentalists (a group of New England reformers, philosophers, and writers, including Ralph Waldo Emerson) formed a club called the Symposium Club. The name again reflects the spirit of discussion, a coming together to share ideas.

synchronous communication A form of on-line communication; real-time communication. With E-MAIL there is a time lag between the sending of a message and its receipt—even more of a time lag, sometimes, between the sending of a message and the reading of it by the intended recipient. Such communication is referred to as asynchronous. With synchronous communication, however, the receiver of the message reads it at the very time that it is being typed and sent into cyberspace. Examples of synchronous communication at the turn of the century were INTERNET relay chat (IRC), sometimes called chat rooms; MOO (multi-user domain, object-oriented); and MUD (multi-user domain).

See also
METAPHOR
PERSONIFICATION
SIMILE

synecdoche A **figure of speech** in which the writer or speaker uses

- a part to stand for the whole
- the whole to stand for a part
- the specific to stand for the general
- the general to stand for the specific
- the material for the thing made from the material

Here are examples of some of the items on the list.

How many hands [i.e., people *or* helpers] do you need to finish the job?
I expect the law [i.e., police officers] to arrive any moment now.
Do you like to tread the boards [i.e., the stage]?

See also
THESAURUS

synonym A word having a similar meaning to another word. *Copy* and *replicate* are synonyms, as are *car* and *automobile*. Use synonyms to vary your DICTION and to make your writing more interesting.

syntax The organization of words, PHRASES, and CLAUSES into SENTENCES. Just one branch of GRAMMAR, syntax refers mainly to sentence structure. When you talk about syntax in your classroom, you may discuss decisions about where to place certain parts of your sentence or why your sentence sounds AWKWARD.

In the following sentences syntax choices can confuse matters—or clear them up.

See also
MISPLACED MODIFIER

> UNCLEAR SYNTAX: I made a cake for my class at school, which was flat and tasteless.

What was flat and tasteless—the class, the school, or the cake?

> CLEAR SYNTAX: For my class at school, I made a cake, which was flat and tasteless.

synthesizing *See* THINKING SKILLS

Set Index

Bold numerals refer to volume numbers. *Italic* volume and page numbers indicate where main entries can be found. Most entries in capital letters signify the building-block terms considered most important for language-arts students. The words in bold identify the eleven categories into which the more than one thousand entries fall. Following each bold term are some of its representative main entries.

oral literature, **1:** 29,
    7: *15–16*
oral presentation, **2:** 5, 6–7,
    4: 35, ***7:*** *16–17*
oral/verbal, 7: 18
order (in writing), **1:** 20,
    7: *18,* 31, **9:** 13, **10:** 81
ordinal number, ***7:*** *18*
organization, name of,
    1: 55, **2:** 15–16, 22, 24,
    4: 80, ***7:*** *20*
organization (of writing),
    7: *20*
orthography. *See* spelling
OUTLINE, **6:** 87, ***7:*** *22–23*
outside of, 7: 20
overgeneralization,
    7: *20–21*
overstatement, ***7:*** *21*
owing to the fact that, 7: 21
oxymoron, ***7:*** *24*

panel discussion, **6:** 44,
    7: *25*
pantomime, ***7:*** *25–26*
paper. *See* book report; five-
    paragraph essay; research
    paper; thesis statement
parable, ***7:*** *26*
paradox, ***7:*** *26*
PARAGRAPH, **3:** 16,
    7: *26–27*
parallelism, **3:** 16,
    7: *26–27*
paraphrase, **6:** 75, ***7:*** *27,
    32,* 60
parentheses, **3:** 22, **6:** 32,
    7: *32–34,* **8:** 22
  with brackets, **2:** 10, **8:** 18,
    19
  with other punctuation,
    3: 68–69, ***7:*** *33–34,*
    43, **8:** 26
parenthetical documentation,
    3: 64–65, 66, ***7:*** *34*
parenthetical expression,
    2: 64, ***7:*** *34*
parody, ***7:*** *34*
participial phrase, ***7:*** *34–35,*
    10: 54
participle, ***7:*** *35–36*
parts of a sentence,
    9: *11–13*
PARTS OF SPEECH,
    7: *38–39*
Parts of Speech. *See*
    adjective, adverb,
    conjunction, interjection,
    noun, preposition,
    pronoun, verb
pass., **5:** 80
passive voice, **1:** 13,
    7: *36–37,* **10:** 64–67
pastoral, ***7:*** *37*
past participle, **5:** 59–63,
    7: *37*
past perfect, overuse of,
    10: 11, 12

past-perfect tense, **5:** 60,
    7: *37, 40,* **10:** 10
past progressive, ***7:*** *87*
past tense, **5:** 59–63, ***7:*** *40,*
    10: 9
peer editing, peer response,
    7: *40,* **10:** 83
pen name, ***7:*** *41*
pentameter, **5:** 18
people/persons, 7: 41
per, 7: 41
percent/percentage, 7: 41
perfect tenses. *See* future-
    perfect tense; past-
    perfect tense; present-
    perfect tense
performance assessment,
    7: *42*
period, **6:** 29, ***7:*** *42–43,*
    8: 21
periodical, **3:** 62, 66, **5:** 35,
    87, ***7:*** *44*
periodic sentence, ***7:*** *43–44*
persecute/prosecute, 7: 45
person, ***7:*** *45–47*
persona, ***7:*** *47,* **9:** 45
personal expression, **10:** 78
personal narrative, ***7:*** *48–49*
personally, 7: 47–48
personal/personnel, 7: 50
personal pronoun, ***7:*** *50,*
    8: 6
personification, **5:** 23,
    7: *50–51*
persuasion, **1:** 26, **6:** 15,
    7: *52,* **10:** 45–46, 79
phoneme, ***7:*** *52–53*
phonetic symbol, ***7:*** *53*
PHRASE, **5:** 43–44, **6:** 46,
    7: *34–35, 7: 56–57,*
    10: 54–55
picaresque novel, **6:** 80, ***7:*** *54*
pictograph, **1:** 38–40,
    7: *54–55*
pie chart (circle graph),
    4: 81, **4:** 86, ***7:*** *55*
place names, ***7:*** *58–59*
plagiarism, **3:** 63, **6:** 75,
    7: *59–60*
planets, stars, heavenly
    bodies, ***7:*** *58–59, 7: 61*
play. *See* drama
plot, **2:** 78–79, ***7:*** *61–62*
plural, **4:** 14, **6:** 56,
    78–79, ***7:*** *63–64,*
    70, 71
p.m. *or* P.M., **5:** 80
poetic device. *See* figurative
    language; sound effects
poetic form, ***7:*** *65–66*
poetic license, ***7:*** *64–65*
poetry, ***7:*** *65–66*
point of view, **6:** 9,
    7: *66–68,* **9:** 18
political term, capitalizing,
    4: 80, **8:** 14
poll, ***7:*** *68*

portfolio, ***7:*** *68–69*
portmanteau word, ***7:*** *69*
Portuguese, **2:** 31, ***7:*** *69*
positive degree, **2:** 74
possessive, **1:** 20, ***7:*** *69–70*
possessive case, **2:** 26–27,
    6: 79, ***7:*** *70–71*
possessive pronoun, **8:** 7
postal service abbreviations,
    1: 5, 14–15
post ergo hoc, **8:** 37
practical writing. *See* E-mail;
    letter, business; memo
precede/proceed, 7: 71
précis. *See* paraphrase;
    summary
PREDICATE, ***7:*** *72–74,*
    9: 12
predicate adjective, **2:** 78,
    7: *75*
predicate noun (predicate
    nominative), **2:** 78,
    7: *75–76*
predicting outcomes, ***7:*** *76*
premise. *See* reasoning
preposition, **4:** 13, ***7:*** *39,*
    7: *79–80*
prepositional phrase, **1:** 17,
    34, **2:** 64, ***7:*** *56–57,*
    7: *80*
present participle, **4:** 77,
    7: *80*
present-perfect form of the
    infinitive, **5:** 43
present-perfect tense, **5:** 60,
    7: *81,* **10:** 9–10
present progressive, ***7:*** *87*
present tense, **5:** *12, 7: 81,*
    10: 8
press release, ***7:*** *81*
pretty, 7: 81
prewriting, ***7:*** *82,* **10:** 80–81
primary source, ***7:*** *83*
principal parts of a verb,
    7: *84,* **10:** 52–53
principal/principle, 7: 85
prior knowledge, building
    on, ***7:*** *85*
problem-and-solution essay,
    7: *85–86*
process, explaining a,
    7: *86–87*
progressive forms of verbs,
    7: *87,* **10:** 10–11
prologue, ***7:*** *87–88*
PRONOUN, ***7:*** 38, **8:** *7–10*
    See also agreement,
    pronoun-antecedent
pronunciation of words,
    1: 9, ***7:*** *53*
proof, **3:** 38, **4:** 29
proofreading, **2:** 25, **8:** *5,
    11,* 12, **10:** 83
propaganda, **8:** *11*

proper adjective, **1:** 20,
    8: *12–13*
proper noun, **1:** 5–6,
    2: 21–24, **6:** 28, 55–56,
    78, **8:** *13–14*
prose, **8:** *15*
protagonist, **6:** 21, **8:** *15*
proverb, **8:** *15*
PSAT/NMSQT, **8:** 81
pseudonym, ***7:*** *41*
publishing, **8:** *15–16,* **9:** 17,
    10: 83–84
Pulitzer Prize, **8:** *16*
pun, **8:** *16–17*
PUNCTUATION,
    6: 29–33, **8:** *18–23*
purple prose, **8:** *17*
purpose for writing, ***7:*** 82,
    8: *17,* **10:** 80
put, **5:** 20–21

quatrain, **8:** *24*
quest (archetype), **8:** *24–25*
question, **5:** 37, 52, 54,
    7: 74
question mark, **5:** 52, **6:** 29,
    8: 21–22, **8:** *25–26*
questionnaire, **8:** *26*
quiet/quit/quite, **8:** *27*
quotation, **1:** 85, **5:** 38, 54,
    6: 75, **8:** *27–28*
quotation mark, **2:** 8, 59,
    4: 72, **8:** 22–23,
    8: *28–30*
quotations, book of, **8:** *30*

rain/reign/rein, **8:** *31*
raise/rise, **8:** *31*
reader-response criticism,
    6: 13
reader-response journal,
    5: 70–71
Readers' Guide, **8:** *32*
readers' theater, ***7:*** 15,
    8: *32–33,* 68–69
reading, **8:** *33–35*
realism, **8:** *35–36*
real/very/really, **8:** *36*
reasoning, **3:** 30–31, **5:** 42,
    7: *20–21,* **8:** *36–37,*
    9: 84
reason is because, **8:** *38*
reason why, **8:** *38*
reciprocal pronoun, **8:** 8,
    8: *38*
redundancy, **3:** 27, ***7:*** 48,
    8: *38–40*
refer/allude, 1: 37
reference, letter of, **8:** *40*
reference, pronoun. *See*
    agreement, pronoun-
    antecedent; pronoun
reference source, **8:** *40–41*
reflecting, **8:** *42,* **10:** 84
reflexive pronoun, **5:** 24,
    8: 7, **8:** *42*
refrain, **2:** 41–42, **8:** *42*